Eclectica Publishing Intl LLC Titles

2004 *Best Fiction Volume One (7th Anniversary)*
2015 *Tales of Choroni*
2016 *Best Poetry Volume One (20th Anniversary)*
2016 *Best Nonfiction Volume One (20th Anniversary)*
2016 *Best Fiction Volume Two (20th Anniversary)*
2016 *Speculative Edition Volume One (20th Anniversary)*

Eclectica Magazine Best Poetry

Celebrating 20 Years Online

Eclectica Magazine Best Poetry

Celebrating 20 Years Online

Selected from *www.eclectica.org*
October 1996 through February 2016
by Jennifer Finstrom

With an Introduction by Jennifer Finstrom and a Foreword by Chris Lott

ECLECTICA PUBLISHING INTL LLC
ALBUQUERQUE, NEW MEXICO

To my Dad, who showed me how to be my own person,
Lori Wojciechowski, my first collaborator in writing,
and all the members of my writing communities.

Acknowledgments

Thanks to...

Eclectica's many readers and many contributors: interacting with you is one of my greatest joys.

Everyone who sends their poems out into the world to find the readers who need them.

Chris Lott for his foreword to this anthology.

The 113 contributors to our Kickstarter campaign who footed the bill for this and three other volumes.

Robert Hoover for providing the cover art for this volume.

Erin Elizabeth Smith, Melvin Sterne, Marilyn Kallet, and Charles Yu for blurbing, but also for their various and substantial contributions to literature, online literature, and/or *Eclectica Magazine*.

Julie King, Pamela Gemin, Mitchel Metz, Carol Fant, and Tara Wynne, who as poetry editors helped select many of these pieces.

The multitude of editors, authors, and supporters not already mentioned above who have helped keep the boat afloat for two decades.

Copyright © 2016 by Eclectica Publishing Intl LLC
Foreword copyright © 2016 by Chris Lott

ALL RIGHTS RESERVED

No part of this work may be reproduced or transmitted in any form or by any means, electronic or mechanical, including photocopying and recording, or by an information storage or retrieval system without the prior written permission of the copyright owner unless such copying is expressly permitted by federal copyright law. With the exception of nonprofit transcriptions in Braille, Eclectica Publishing Intl LLC is not authorized to grant permission for further uses of copyrighted selections reprinted in this book without the permission of their owners. Permission must be obtained from the individual copyright authors as identified herein. Email queries and requests for permission to make copies of Eclectica Publishing Intl LLC material to editors@eclectica.org.

Visit our website at www.eclectica.org.

ISBN 978-0-9968830-1-6

Printed in the United States of America

All works originally published in *Eclectica Magazine* (www.eclectica.org) and reprinted by permission of the authors.

Contents

Foreword

THE VOLUME YOU now hold in your hands is remarkable for its very ordinariness. Consider: you are about to read a selection of poems in a book—a technology so old and commonplace, most of us don't even remember it *is* a technology—drawn from a publication produced using one of the newest and most transformative technologies of our time, the web... which presents itself, for the most part, in the form of something older than either of them, the scroll.

Consider also: it took more than three centuries for the codex to replace the scroll, for cubbyholes and scribes to be pushed out of the way in favor of shelves and movable type. The public web, the "World Wide" prefix now redundant and the capitalization unnecessary, has existed for fewer than 25 years, but already the virtual town criers of the hype cycle have announced the deaths and resurrections of the book and the ebook alike.

In this context, *Eclectica Magazine*—celebrating a 20th birthday I never could have imagined when I created the first issue on my Windows 95 PC and slowly pushed it through the straw of a 9600 baud modem—has been extraordinarily long-lived. For that reason alone, a celebratory anthology is warranted. But there's more.

The idea of the anthology, the *need* for them, was borne of a culture of scarcity. It was impractical for all but the richest Greeks to collect a significant portion of the poetry scrolls from which Meleager of Gadara gathered selections nearly 2,000 years ago for the now lost *Anthologia* that gives us these collections' common name. Anthologies gave readers and more importantly, performers and their large audiences, a glimpse of an otherwise inaccessible, even literally incomprehensible landscape most had neither the resources nor the ability to experience for themselves.

But even then, the seeds for our contemporary culture of abundance had been sown. Already it was impossible for any but the most ardent, learned specialist to read or listen widely enough to make a reasonably representative selection. Now, the free, wholly volunteer-created Project Gutenberg library of online texts alone rivals, in quantity, the Great Library of Alexandria... and the entire collection fits easily on my phone. And that's a drop in the proverbial bucket of books available through Google Books and the Internet Archive, themselves emptying continuously into a veritable sea of online publications, ebooks, and databases.

In a culture of abundance, the anthology remains a means of wayfinding, sense-making, and taste-defining. In the grand scheme of things, the 20-year run of—and mere thousands of poems to be found in—*Eclectica* may be small, but for the reader browsing its archives the prospect looms large. Hence the timeliness of anthologies like this one. It's not inconceivable that some future student will look back at what *Eclectica* published (promoted, wrought, spawned) and refer to the Eclectican poets in the same way they speak of the Georgian poets, as if the collections they appeared in comprised a material location. And so such anthologies did, at least in the geography of the readers' imagination, notional but very real places not that different from the digital space where *Eclectica* lives and breathes now.

Eclectica is a virtual land of a thousand links (in fact, 44,353 of them as I write this) whose borders change, Heisenbergian style, not just with every new issue but with the perspective of every reader. An intrepid explorer may start at any point and create as many routes through this burgeoning world as time allows. Alfred Korzybski famously noted "a map is not the territory it represents," but most sources inconveniently leave off the second half of his observation, that a map "if correct, has a similar structure to the territory, which accounts for its usefulness." This 20th anniversary anthology is both a well-earned celebration of an eminent publication and a convenient, portable starting point for your journey, a (thankfully finite) guide to *Eclectica's* ever-expanding, sometimes magical territory.

Chris Lott co-founded Eclectica Magazine. He continues to live, work, teach, and write in Fairbanks, Alaska.

Introduction

NEAR THE END of 1999, I received an email from Julie King, then poetry editor of *Eclectica Magazine,* and a poet whose work I admired very much. I don't remember the specific wording of that email, but Julie was asking me to submit several poems to *Eclectica* for possible inclusion as a Spotlight feature, which did in fact appear in the January/February issue of 2000. I truly couldn't have been more delighted. At that time, I might have had two or three poems appearing in print literary journals, but the feature in *Eclectica* would be my first foray into online publishing. Not all of my family had Internet access at that time, and every now and again I still come across a printed copy of those poems that I had meant to give someone. And when my grandmother died in 2010, some copies of those poems were among the papers and cards my aunts returned to me.

A year passed, and Julie emailed me again. This time, it was regarding the brand new Word Poem Special Feature, now an *Eclectica* mainstay and one of my favorite things. She was asking me—and several other poets—to provide a quarterly contribution and write a word poem. She provided the four words to me, and over the next several years, I contributed a word poem to almost every issue. If nothing else, this insured I was writing at least four poems a year. At this time in my life, I was waiting tables full time, working on a novel, and occasionally sending out poems for possible publication, more and more frequently to online publications. I would work on the poems at the restaurant, writing the four words over and over on order slips and paper menus, dashing away to the break room when I got an idea.

I begin this introduction with my own first memories of *Eclectica* for a couple of reasons. One, and possibly the most important, is that becoming involved with *Eclectica*—as a contributor first and then as poetry editor in 2005—introduced me to what it was like to be a part of a vibrant community of writers. I had read *Eclectica* for many years before joining the staff, and I saw many names repeated over and over (several of those names appear in this volume as well). As I began to read other online literary journals, I would see those same names repeated. I read the work of those poets with an increasing sense of the person on the other side of the words. I read bios and tried to imagine if the life on the other end resembled mine with its scribbled poems on pizza order slips. I had spent so much time writing on my own that finding writers out there in the world was a revelation I've carried firmly with me into other areas of my life.

Writing is always better with other people, and I'm not even sure when some of those writers I interacted with online became writer friends. I do remember putting together the July/August 2010 volume from a hotel in Ann Arbor where I was staying while my mother was in intensive care and where she died that fall. The issue still went out, and I remember being grateful I had that editing work to do. I'm sure I wrote a few personal notes to contributors, telling them where I was and why as I sent their acceptances.

Another reason I began here with my own introduction to *Eclectica* is because I'd like to say something about how publishing has changed since the very first issue in 1996 to now—and how it will still continue to change. In the late 1990s, I could not have predicted how different the world would look today: just as today, I can't picture what a future 20 years from now would resemble. I know there will be many changes in how we communicate and how poems are reaching readers in the world. I try to envision a 40-year anniversary anthology, and beyond knowing it would contain amazing work, I can't begin to describe it.

In 1996, I was still buying each new yearly edition of *Poets Market* and memorizing how query letters should look and everything about SASEs. I've dropped many a submission into the corner mailbox, wishing it well and not knowing if it would safely reach its destination. I like the publishing world that we have now ever so much better, and I can't wait to see what the future holds, both for publishing and for *Eclectica*.

The poems here are arranged intuitively, and they seem to me to "belong" where they are in the collection. That isn't to say that if I arranged them again in a year, I wouldn't see a world of new connections and confluences and end up with something that could be read completely differently. But let's look at where the first poem starts us out and where the last poem leaves us. The poem that begins the anthology is Rachel Dacus's "My Wishing Star on a Long Ride," and the title alone seems apropos to start off such a collection. I feel we are alone here with the night sky, and "I have hooked my star / to dawn's grapefruit moon" is an apt beginning. The ending seems to me just as appropriate, and if we began at dawn, the collection ends with John Ladd Zorn's "Coast Starlight, Northbound," and though this poem seems to take place during daylight hours, I always read it with a sense of the night, particularly the end where "Past clusters of deadwood / Tangled like lost souls—/ The Inferno open on my lap." We began, as readers, on a horse, but ended as a passenger on a train. In both instances, we are carried along by a force outside of ourselves, and this, too, seems particularly fitting.

I love writing and I love being a writer, but what I love more than either of those things is working with writers. I do this as a teacher and a tutor, but my identity as a poetry editor is also a big part of who I am. Putting this anthology together is by far one of the most challenging things I've ever done. Reading through 20 years of work was wonderful and overwhelming and inspiring, and that doesn't even begin to discuss the poem choice process, which was itself amazing and difficult and heartbreaking. I dearly love every poem in this volume, and I love so many poems that aren't here.

And of course, I want to leave you with the knowledge that the true "director's cut" of this anthology is our staggeringly impressive online archives. If you find a poet in this volume whose work you love, chances are you'll find another one or two or a dozen poems waiting for you there. And while I hope our ever-growing archives is where this anthology will lead you, even more than that, I hope it makes you pause for a moment and think about the communities of writers in your life. Truly, no community of writers can be too large, and I hope this one that we are all a part of will just continue to grow.

RACHEL DACUS

My Wishing Star on a Long Ride

from July/August 2015

That last summer we sat
in creaking saddles on day trips
in the High Sierra, inhaling petrichor
and lichened bedrock.
Nudged cattle through tall grass.

I had all I ever wanted, at thirteen:
my own horse and a long August.
Above the cabin, stars buzzing
like mosquitoes. I knew the seasons
to come wouldn't have horses and those stars.

This morning above my town trees gallop
in the wind, flexing thin branches,
gold leaves whipping around
themselves like a horse
that bucks when backing up.

I have hooked my star
to dawn's grapefruit moon.
Boughs creak like saddles
in the wind. My wishing star, gone
on a long ride, vanished in a meteor shower.

The news said a chance of more
showers later. That made me buck
and back up at a sudden call
from lost mountains. At sixty-five,
I spun around, pranced downhill

in a last sweet lope to the valley
of lost things, where a new trail starts
and the underground river cuts
deeper, flashing its dark lights.

CLARE L. MARTIN

Eating the Heart First

from January/February 2008

Her body bristles.
She hears the plucked string,
the whoosh of arrow—

When she is felled,
you must eat the heart first.

It is a hellish flower.
Cut it out whole. Its pulse fills your hand.

She will talk in your skin.
Her fear will mingle with your own.

Cold, you sleep.
Your dreams flood with moons.

Wolves hunt the night of your mind,
keep you running.

JARED CARTER

The Philosopher's House

from October/November 2008

It is abandoned, and it stands by itself
in a field of high grass sifted by the wind.

It is old, it is made of maple and walnut,
it consists of many rooms, all empty now.

You can walk up on the porch, you can peer
through the windows. There is nothing inside.

And yet it is peaceful, it is obvious that work
was once done here. There are no distractions.

There is nothing in excess. An old guidebook,
long out of print, persuaded you to come here.

There is a stone barn, half sunk in the hillside,
with bales of hay stacked in the dusty haymow.

This was home for the philosopher and his wife.
He had many thoughts, and he wrote them down.

Now, there is only the wind and the gray barn,
and this empty house, that seems to be waiting.

Farther on is the river that does not seem to be
waiting at all, but moves along at its own pace.

The philosopher wondered about such matters—
whether all things are in motion, or at rest.

That may be why he chose to live in this place,
here in this field of high grass sifted by the wind.

HEATHER STYKA

Amateur Astronomer

from October/November 2009

In grade school, I avoided displaying my knowledge
of dark matter and particle accelerators, betraying
my father, who had taught me such things
during bike rides past Fermilab.

When I visit, he comes up from the basement
with piles of tapes: late-night PBS specials
on black holes, supernovae. I analyze
the voice, spewing data with movie-trailer
intonation, background music littered with
augmented triads, those unnerving sounds
that belong behind old silent films,
organ cueing villains or asteroids.

My father drives off at ungodly hours
in search of dark, open fields, telescope
buckled up in the back seat of his truck.

When he brings me with him, we see
different skies. He was weaned on
too much *Star Trek* or Bradbury,
navigates with a red pocket flashlight
and a star map. He says Andromeda
is the nearest galaxy to Earth.
I remind him that she is Cassiopeia's daughter.

JOHN REINHARD

Signing Away Your Death

from October/November 2002

Seeing both of her parents dead at 76
my granny at 75 began
to make plans. She was certain
her shadow would soon belong to the moon
instead of the sun, so
she asked the sons and daughters, all
the grandkids, a few friends
to lay claim to everything
she owned. We were instructed
to ignore my grandfather and
sign our names to whatever in the house
we wanted. Mirrors, photos, tables, chairs.
My aunt Ann signed the piano. Uncle Terry
almost everything else, but we learned
his signature could be erased.
I signed my name to four bottles of Crown Royal.

At 76, her death in sight, maybe
walking down Easterday Avenue in late fall, Granny
started actually giving away her signed things.
If my grandfather complained, she'd give him
a drink or tell him to cook dinner, although
she'd already given me his favorite pan.

At 77, she began wondering
what went wrong. Why did the air
continue to sting and soothe her northern nights.
In her 80s, the walls must have seemed bare,
especially in winter when the light almost
collapsed though the sky sometimes burned.
In her 80s, she signed away her husband,
a granddaughter, her left breast. Signed away
countless friends genuine and otherwise. Signed
away great distances and niceties and picnics by the big lake.

Her final weeks, at 90, were down to a frame of house, whiskey
and Canada Dry, and drives to the river where
she refused to sign away the freighters or me,
though she took great delight in finally
signing away the gulls and the feathery drifts
of their persistent screeks.

And now she's become nothing
more than the space
where the rest of the world lives.
I sign my name to that
every day. To tree, brook,
and track of snow. To the laughing
mouths of my own children. To my own
dying, somewhere north of the Brooks Range
as I write this, and moving
very deliberately south. And I think
often of how practiced my granny's hand
and signature became
in the many years after her death, as
she signed away, for keeps, and we signed on.

LAURA MADELINE WISEMAN

Picking for Silver at the Matilda Fletcher Mine, 1895

from October/November 2010

It ticked the man off, just a little, the crotch-high boots,
the carbide lamp, the slick jacket, the wet hat,
the dank smell of men bathed in last night's beer.

Sure he had his broom and pick axe, his chisel,
the metal pail of lunch he'd prepared himself
this morning at six. But most men didn't study

to be a mining engineer, a job that didn't exist
in Reward Gold or in this century's Mayflower.
$10,000 had been made here in 1879. In 1895

as he heaved three hours' work into a cart,
he coughed, a reminder of childhood disease,
of how the mind can make you ill with a thought.

What he wanted was to be a man, to marry
his college sweetheart, to earn a million at 30.
His mother had died at 35. His father, at 34. At 21

and at $2.50 a day, he'd never amount to much
more than the wayward flow of ruby and lead,
silver and gray copper. But he needed to

watch for the telltale rumble of another cave-in
over Georgetown in the Democrat mountains
like the one in 1884, the year of his mother's death.

It was always possible to be smothered and crushed,
to swallow the dirt, water, and rock of Colorado.
He hoped to exit the mouth of Matilda Fletcher alive

and again feel the curious tug of something. More
than inward silence, as if after all these years
of waiting, he knew he now had something to say.

PENELOPE SCAMBLY SCHOTT

Spring Housecleaning

from July/August 2007

I am sorting through a cupboard of skeletons:
the giving flesh I used to touch has fallen away,
the pretty boy whose smell I breathed for lunch.

I am sorting through odd drawers of notions:
a hundred, hundred tiny silver thimbles stashed,
or what is prophesied by seeing thirteen crows.

But mostly today I am sorting through words:
Everything shabby or chipped or out-of-date
gets set on a table for my coming garage sale.

There you have *soup tureen, concupiscence,*
insurmountable grief. Here you have *bobeche*
for catching candle drips, *pianoforte, shame.*

I'll bargain: take two, and the third comes free.
I'd meant to set out *pincushion, darning egg,*
but then I couldn't seem to live without them,

just as I still need *williwaw*, that terrible polar
squall.

GEORGE MOORE

What We Want

from October/November 2009

The pigs are up early this morning
hording toward some invisible enemy or friend,
or to the troughs that are filled this time each day
as day breaks open like a ripe husk of damp seed,
and the pigs are greedy, but this greed is their
kind, the movement of their selves through
all time, the name they are known by,
the thing they do that distinguishes
hunger.

And from across the field at the house,
I want juice with my morning tea, I want quiet
ripening like the moon in its seed pod, I want
the other world than the one I have created,
the world that waits perpetually until my death,
I want more than I have before me at this moment,
want to be heard and felt, the words to flow
like milk from the teats of the pigs
into their waiting young.

NOAH ENGEL

A Turtle in my Backyard

from January/February 2015

I bent down
to look at
a turtle
that crept into
my backyard
she was hiding
so I pretended not to look
instead I was writing
this poem
when my dog
runs over with her
in his mouth
her shell scratched
he was happy about it
I couldn't look at her
but I did
I saw her face
inside of her shell
her eyes
were blue

ERIKA LUTZNER

The Great Mother Has No Face

from January/February 2010

For Wisława Szymborska

Do you believe in rebirth?
the goat asked the stone as they lay
by the river taking in the noonday heat

goat and stone

stone pillowing goat
goat protecting stone

river gently flowing past
future meeting in the middle of yesterday

stone turns to goat, were we family before
we knew each other?

goat contemplates for a moment,
we've known each other before God
existed, before the creation of moons,
I am blood, you are bone—

SVETLANA LAVOCHKINA

A Disaster

from October/November 2010

Translated from the work of Vasyl Holoborodko

For lack of money
my apartment is still unfurnished—
the books are lined up against the wall in piles,
like in a Japanese student's room.

They have been there for so long
that I got used to such an interior,
and can easily find the book I need.

(Epiphany:
books in their usual places
are a symbol, by definition, of
"something that brings about serenity.")

But if by chance I misplace a book, suddenly,
everything changes—
the height of the pile, and even the other piles.
The interior changes.
It also changes
if I put a garden spade against the wall.
All this changes my whole life:
it takes me so much time to find the book I need

that I can find no more time to look out the window
to admire a blossoming cherry-tree
by the house across the street.
It is impossible to return to the initial state—
I don't know what the order was
in the piles along the wall
before the disaster.

(Epiphany:
misplaced books are a symbol,
by definition, of
"something that causes anxiety.")

Now, where shall I look for my Shevchenko?
Where shall I look for my Sachenko?

TAYLOR GRAHAM

High Lakes

from April/May 2013

Three German Shepherds in an open jeep
on the bumpiest road.
Not a road, just somebody's sketch
of how to get from highway to the heart
of wilderness. My arms
around my two dogs, Jerry's dog lying
heavy on my feet; search gear gathered in
a hurry, stashed wherever it fit.
The jeep-jolt knocking my bones out of
whack.
And on this July morning, the vault
of heaven was a blue lake thin on oxygen.
I hadn't had much sleep. The call
just after midnight:
fisherman missing on a lake distant-blue.
Map showed a whole string of lakes,
like charms on a girl's bracelet.
Would we ever arrive at the right one;
get out of this jeep
so I could set out searching with my dog?
On the long dark drive up-
valley, up-mountain, a planet winked at me
through windshield, just left of Orion
and his trusty dog Sirius.
Let them, from their much higher vantage
point, join our search.

TIM HAWKINS

Elegy within Earshot of Howling

from April/May 2012

For Todd Tubergen

Returning from a family birding trip to Manistee,
I finally found your grave after all these years.

About to give up in my third pass through the small country
cemetery,
I caught my breath as I literally stumbled upon your name.

Like you, the marker was slightly off kilter,
and, as if in deference to the memory of your style,
it wore the five o'clock shadow of a decade of wind and rain.

My four-year-old ran laughing around your stone
while his older brother doled out harsh glares and whispers
of reprimand, until I patted him on the shoulder to say it was all
right.

As we stood there in the midst of that sweet laughter
and the beginnings of a soft spring rain,
I remembered the last time we spoke on the phone,
very near the end, when you invoked Rilke:

> Take the emptiness you hold in your arms
> and scatter it into the open spaces we breathe:
> maybe the birds will feel how the air is thinner
> and fly with more affection...

and announced your love for all
the youthful, scattered days of our friendship
when we ran from place to place, from one illicit dawn to the
next,
down to the continent's edge
to shout wild oaths and promises.

Your voice was so thin and rasping,
it foretold, without proclaiming, the inevitable,
so different than what we had promised and imagined.
"Beauty is nothing but the beginning of terror, which we are still
just able to endure,"
I somehow managed to respond.

When we hung up that last time, my wife held me down
as I howled and raged on my hands and knees
all across the cold, hard tiles of that floor on another continent,
as worms crawled beneath the foundation of our house
and stars blazed outside in the night sky.

For a while I tried to follow your advice
and even pledged to serenade
each of the mornings after you died
with some form or another
of my ragged and lusty song.

But my voice has grown hoarse and I am forgetful—
still I'm aware of some of what remains,
aware now that I've set up camp, without even knowing it,
in the proximity of birds, and within earshot of that howling,
with ready and certain access to the reverberations of its call.

TERESA WHITE

Rag Cutting

from September/October 1999

I sat with Betty
at the steel monster six feet high,
a two-seater calliope with blades
on either side,
and felt like the princess in Rumpelstiltskin
with straw to spin
though we had a mountain of coveralls
to cut into rags before nightfall.
Cheaper than paper towels for the gas
stations that bought them,
we couldn't cut fast enough.
There was a science to it;
Betty taught me well:
off went the collars with a zip,
followed by the sleeves in two steps.
We cut the sleeves in half
before we cut the front from back.
The legs were next with just a few
steps and then we started over again.
I would have slipped and cut myself
but Betty kept me alert
talking all day about her old man.
"If I keep the dishes done and the bed
made, Harold will love me up two, maybe
three times a week," she said,

or "be sure and feed your man
red meat—it'll keep him sexual."
She was a newlywed at forty-five,
proud to share her advice with me,
down on my luck at twenty-three.
Day in, day out, week after week:
off went a collar, off went a sleeve.

PAUL HOSTOVSKY
To Leave
from October/November 2007

Those rocky outcroppings
on the side of the highway
remind me of the planets
the Little Prince visited—

just big enough
for one person and a desk,
a space for thinking to yourself
out in the middle of space,

I think to myself as I drive past,
picturing that little kid
with the long scarf and yellow hair
standing up there. How did he

get around anyway? They never
explained that in the book. Madame
loved that book and wanted us
to love it, too. But I think we

misunderstood it. Something about
a flower and a sheep. A fox and a hat that
was really a snake with an elephant
inside it. That book was harder

than it looked. Maybe that's why
I'm still thinking about it now,
looking for an exit ramp, light-years
away from the hillocky sphere where I was a kid

myself once. Madame got sick—
and we had a substitute teacher then
who dropped her r's, even in French.
Every time she dropped an r we dropped

a book, loudly on the floor. Oh, how we
tortured her. She got mad, ordered me to
leave: *Sortez!* Minus the r, it sounded
like *sauter*: to jump. So I jumped

up and down, up and down. I kept
jumping because she kept on yelling:
Sautez! Sautez! Madame never did
come back. I think she may have

died. It was ambiguous, the way
they left it at the end of that book—you felt
like crying though it wasn't clear exactly
what happened. Just that it was sad,

but also somehow very
beautiful. Sometimes you don't
quite know why you feel like crying.
You just do. And it feels good, somehow.

Once upon a time I was laughing,
when the next thing I knew
a book shut loudly, then a door
was closing behind me

and I was leaving—
walking down an infinitely tessellating
hallway, crying
with a little jump in my step.

LEEANN PICKRELL

Between Market and Mission

from July/August 2008

At the café on Market, a woman
in her friend's arms, a sadness I
recognize—by the way her body
weeps—as feeling endless.

Coffee in hand, I step wide to
avoid the puddle formed from
three days of rain still falling. I walk

one block, my umbrella unfurled.
On my shoulders, I carry my life
and my work. At Mission, a man on a bike

crosses with the traffic as I wait for
the light to change. He smiles and I forget
my usual caution and smile too. He turns
around then, rides up to pause beside me.

"I want to tell you three things," he says.
"One, you're really cute. Two, your
shoe's untied, and three, have a good weekend."

On a Friday afternoon, even on this
flat expanse of one city block, I walk
an edge between grief and possibility.

ROHITH SUNDARARAMAN

As a grandfather waits to meet

from January/February 2008

his grandson after six years, he
sits on the wheezing rocking chair
propped by the door, and whenever
a car passes by the window, his
smoke-wisp eyebrows curl into waves.
With eyeglasses left dangling at
the chest and hands folded over
his lap, he leans forward to meet
his watch every five minutes. As a rush
of air leaks through his lips, he
eases back into the chair, tiny transparent
fish swim from the twin pools of his eyes,
each time a little closer to the sun.

KIMBERLY L. BECKER

The girl on the train

from October/November 2007

to Venice is asleep with her lithe
legs drawn up,
her bare feet propped
under the window.
Her head is bowed
like a swan's to its plumage
we think, self-conscious of our thought.

Before, when the girl had gone to pee,
her mother had confided that her daughter is a swimmer
and on her way to meet her boyfriend from Slovenia.
She (the mother) is banking on a break-up.

As the train nears the station
the girl, flushed and almost beautiful, rouses
and blinks, guileless against the light
and the heat,
forgetting altogether for a moment
that she is in another country
from the one she recently inhabited in dreams.

We forget with her, borne as we are over water into this city of
    water
atop rotting pilings
(all our dreams are ever built on).
Still they hold.

SANDY ANDERSON

Stranger

from October/November 2011

I was in the middle of the divorce
when a stranger walked in
and took my place.
At first I was disoriented,
after all this was my pain,
my loss. But the more I watched her
the more relieved I was.
She made all the stupid concessions
I always had, so I left her alone.
My husband, or should I say ex,
never noticed the difference.
I found this a bit perturbing,
but now I was free, and that life
belongs to somebody else.

SARAH YOST

When We Learned to Be Chameleons

from October/November 2009

we kept all things special in secret boxes of flesh and bone
suspended in little squares of liquid silence, hidden
from adults, whose colorless eyes could dry up whole seas
of inky mystique. we learned. we learned to look on
either side of ourselves and quite seamlessly fade from
magenta to puce. we learned to creep very slowly in
conversation, to keep the cupboards closed tightly
when company was over, smile and take the cookies
offered us—please & thank you, curtsey, ma'am—and walk
along the curb, keeping clear of the muck-muddy, leaf-clotted
gutters, those veins of our pounding hearts, until they too dried
to dust and blew away, and our little boxes, we buried as coffins

JESSE DAMIANI

After Another Day Spent on the Couch

from October/November 2011

I can't hussy here—it's too loud. Water
drips from cracks in the ceiling.
The borrowed wi-fi is on the fritz
& the entire world is in flux. I imagine
paradigms rotating in slow motion.
Mania. Buildings erupt at such
deliberate speeds you can see the fire
spark from air—nothing. I can't cowl
shadow here. I can't desk drawer.
On TV, there's an old married couple
on a bench. One hand touches another
& can't you just imagine the wedding
ceremony? The two of them all fluo-
rescent shine. Imagine a time lapse
of their skin mottling with age. Finality,
or the semblance thereof. I'm here
alone because I can't compete
with the clear eyes of strangers. If you
get this message, please believe me:
I can't cartography. I can't toaster oven.

FRANK VAN ZANT

Pete Reiser & the Ebbet's Outfield Wall

from January/February 2000

Remember Pete like a half-smoked ballpark stogy
stuck in the ashtray wall
at 340 feet or so,
the tip of his head with flame expiring,
smoke streaming out of him.

Not like today's millionaire reserve
who'd hesitate, be able to play tomorrow,
Reiser sacrificed himself
like a soldier diving on a live grenade,
or a caught spy facing a squad of guns
but clutching with his heart-nerve
that white stitched secret.

TOM SHEEHAN

Cutting Ice on Rapid Tucker's Pond

from July/August 2001

It was always horses, dragging ice
to the wooden ramp obeying chugs
of the gasoline engine, their traces
often slack as the ice slid on ice
and thundered slowly and resolutely
from hard shore to hard shore. Up the
ramp the ice cakes lumbered, six feet
of Arctic beauty before the huge saw
found the blue and silver-red signals
sitting just under cover and waiting
to flash once more before sawdust
poured down on their frantic coloring.
I have no hard memory of the men who
steamed their labors on the hard pond,
who swore and drank coffee from bottles
whiskey belonged in, who went gloveless
and carefree and irreverent to winter.
Of their faces I have no memory, or names,
or how they spent their money downtown,
or where they trod for stitches when
the angry saw went haywire. I only know
they poled ice floes and huge cakes

with an indifferent touch, that they argued
long hours against the cold, the wind,
and the incessant and desperate need
for sleep, that at zero degrees they mopped
brows with red kerchiefs large as sails.
They were the reverse itinerants
who came not for fruit but for ice drop,
who appeared one Saturday in December
and began to take away pieces of our pond,
huge rectangular chunks they hitched
up to horses shrouded wholly in steam,
their wide mouths rimmed by thick lips
often white with frost around the red tongues.
They wore soft felt hats, brimmed, jackets
so odd you could not find a mate, but boots
with horsehide laces, wide belts, and looked
westward where the sun would set part-ways
through the afternoon.

In latest July, ever,
you could find December deep in the icehouse
under the waves of orange sawdust still wet
with some of their sweat, a cool hideaway
to puff the stub of a cigarette, touch a breast,
play hide and seek for hours as winter
sprawled under our feet cold and foreboding
and nearly two floors high inside redan walls
two feet thick.

Mostly I remember the eyes
of a horse who plunged through the ice,
like great dishes of fear, wide and frightened
and full of the utmost knowledge. His front
hooves slashed away at the ragged rim of ice,
but could not lift him out, or leather traces
or ropes or sixty feet of chain, and when he
went down, like a boat plunging, huge bubbles
burst on the surface and a December afternoon
became quiet.

We stood transfixed, as if frozen
in the gray of that day, the itinerant workers,
other horses at rest, my shod friends, as Rapid
Tucker's Pond began its disappearance under
the edge of yesterday.

KATHRYN T. S. BASS

Sometimes You Do Something Before It Happens

from April/May 2002

I know when I open my mouth I will start
the conversation that will end everything
we knew before.

We have held our breath to prevent this.

I know this is where it will happen: our
botanic gardens; that the sound of my words,
the hard, irreversible, until now unspoken
truth, will dwell here for you among the lavender
and English thyme and lamb's ears (so
soft) and rosemary, which you
always remember is for remembrance.

Broken, like the silence, we will walk away
from the warm light, the dotted Spring sky,
the reticulated ivy, the knot garden, suddenly
untied, and you will begin, and I will
begin, to create our separate stories
of the break up, our hollowed-out chests not
showing the concave shell blown out between us.

You will walk away, believing
that we have a later we can meet in. I will try
to love you at arms' length, then, and remember
with this emptiness, how you filled me, almost

enough. But maybe this is not the time, the time

that's coming. Maybe in this moment, as you bury
your round and generous face in the full pink peony (a beautiful
cabbage of a flower), as you risk inhaling a dozen courting ants,
seeking its sweet, sweet abundance, I think maybe
I will say nothing, nothing sharper
than those vivid petals, that spherical bloom. I nose

into a flower myself: it so supple, even the edges feel smooth,
so stiff; it seems to bear my weight, bend rightly,
and bounce back, holding again its perfect shape.

LAIRD BARRON

Sawgrass

from July/August 2004

I saw you
Before I saw them
Red-lipped as if they had gnawed you
Each one fat from staring
At the great black stake

Crowds dispersed as tall clouds do
With small claps and thin forks
Crossing
Some claimed Christ called down, late
I saw you
You were the same as always
Your hand on your hip
Straw from the field floating
In a halo

I saw you yesterday
I asked this soft ground that folds my shadow
How does the green eat
Everything so quickly?
Today I found your bonnet in high grass
Where the road ends
I saw some birds rising

CY DILLON

Night Drive

from January/February 2009

Seen from the ridgeline above
Ground fog in hollows and along streams
Pulls the unexpected
From the familiar sleeve of night

A shadow memory
        vaguely threatening
Those headlights gaining from behind
        on an empty highway

Blind speed is no escape
Nor is fear
Enter the lost clouds humbly
A traveler
Come home to a changed land

ARLENE ANG

Afternoon Stroll

from January/February 2008

The street is familiar:
almond trees, a stone sculpture
on the lawn, the grass
overwhelmed by forget-me-not.

Birds in the sky appear
like V-cut antennae. A car honks.
Leather shoes on gravel: someone
comes through the front door. Slam.

In my left pocket, a crumpled
receipt for twelve eggs—purple ink
lost in the washer. Wind like the cold
towel I applied on her forehead.

The sun is strangely out.
It's one of those days that make me
wish I have a hat: everyone
will be wondering where I've gone.

Funeral is at five. Years before
she said I shouldn't attend, urged me
to wear red. Her topaz breastpin
on my dress lends a warm twinkle.

WILLIAM LANTRY

Home

from October 1996

"If I didn't tell her, I could leave today..." —??

Whiteness of fog covers our August fields,
cold rain again. A gray car leaves the road.
Deer begin to blossom on edges,
or perch on yellow lines.
Blackbirds convene. A few green leaves
predict the elms in weeks.
Somewhere I've seen this before.
Just another place on the continent.
But the land has ending.
Fire is the awkward message there.
The smoke white sky, ash gray on our road,
or yellow clothes on moonscapes,
my shovel turning embers.
There was a time to leave.
But there is no time to return.
I do not build bronze monuments.
Warmth is not absence of cold,
desert sand is snow. Our wings
cannot converge on what has never been.
After long waiting, elms remake themselves.
And she is here, not on some distant shore.

MIHIR VATSA

Going to the Rain

from July/August 2013

At New Delhi Station
the commands are always unclear
so we spy on the brakes
of an outbound train—

New Delhi Sealdah Special
via Koderma.

Once inside
we realize there's no water
two more hours
and there's no light.

We joke on the efficiency
of the Indian Railway
our faces showing borders
from the sweat
so if you ask someone
they will sing

We are going to the rain!

Tomorrow
we will find warmth
somewhere else
because

regardless of the months
we are always leaving Delhi.

Some men laugh at this.

In the evening, the wheels
roar over an underfed river

the moon sticks to the bars
on our windows, spurring
us to stretch the nightfall.

Outside
a hundred cities fall in the dark.

MICHAEL VANCALBERGH

Dear Kristin,

from October/November 2002

I am writing you a poem. I know, it looks like a letter, but trust me. This is a poem trapped inside a letter that is actually a poem looking like a letter. I can make it look like a poem if you don't believe me:

> cleaning my desk of dust
> there are
> feelings of retribution,
> wiping away
> those things I should have done and
> said

I want to assure you that this is truly what it is, a poem. I stress this because letters are fleeting and polite, but poems are True. Letters pass with red hands in circles. Poems exist in space, expanding. Letters live and die. No, letters are dead before. Poems are Elijah. Letters are Congratulations! Poems are This is closer to your beginning. In the end we all want Poems.

Happy Birthday,

Mike

JULIE KING

Natural History

from November 1996

Study the origin of us.
You, prone to sinus infections,
wore a coat too heavy
for the weather. You carried
a shotgun and a jackrabbit,
swinging it like a lantern.
I was attracted to your silhouette,
the illusion of bulk and light.

So here we are. Study the evolution
of us. I sit on the porch, swinging
a bottle of Cuervo, watching phoenix
skip across the mesa, too quick
for their little bones. You wear
the tattered coat, cough phlegm
hot as chili peppers, slap
a rabbit on the cutting board.

What do you make of this study,
the interrelationship of organisms,
our own natural history? You gut
the rabbit with one slice, sure
of the precision of the knife,
the thick blood of the kill.

(Poem selected for inclusion by Tom Dooley)

PAMELA GEMIN

I Remember How This Song Goes

from October/November 2002

Two beers and a hurricane, twenty years piss away,
and when John comes back from the bar with another
big red drink, it might as well be the Del Rio circa 1979, but no
it's the Velvet Dog, New Orleans, 21st Century. Alcohol
whispers where you been girl we've missed you welcome back.
Josie asks who wants to play a drinking game called "I Never";

the darer tells something she's never done, like *I've never*
smoked angel dust, and those who have done that sin have to hoist
 away.
Paula says honey count me out, but I'll bet we're all thinking back.
I love the little gold lights on the ceiling, and I'd love another
big red drink. I love those jangly guitars splashing out of the juke,
 guitars
of fried oysters, ripped fingernails, rhinestone crowns—I know

this song—*I feel the horses coming galloping*—I remember, I know
what comes next, jangling guitars playing into the bridge—*I will never*
grow old   I'll go to heaven tonight   There is a storm in the form of a girl
and a high-heeled boy in black-feather boa skateboarding away.
He's left a half-pack of Newports on the bar, and if I have another
red drink I'll be smoking again, snap out of it snap but it's coming
 back
home and there's never been anyplace like it. Grateful to breathe back
the smoke of a hundred lit cigarettes, I smile over at John, who knows

and remembers me best like this, in the sparkly pretty lights of let's
have another,
quick before it melts to lost keys lost cars smeared lashes neverland
payphones odd bruises bare feet sliced on broken glass; and I've been
away,
but *I feel the horses coming galloping I'll go to heaven tonight*

BRENT FISK

The House on Gypsy Ridge

from October/November 2009

My grandmother's moods turned liquid,
black as the ink of squids. Chameleon in a nightgown,
she'd scramble eggs for one too many plates.
His empty chair would rock her.

Cobwebs in the cupboards of her heart,
embers of the woodstove, the smoke
that spins away when a candle is put out.

The house held together
with toothpaste spit, the mud from our boots,
the spindly legs of silverfish. She teetered
atop the step ladder, shook the husks
of ladybugs from the globes of ceiling lamps.

She'd wring the grime from the rags of his shirts
and wipe the dust from lamp cords and table legs.
She wiped our faces raw and swept the darkness
down the cellar stairs. She beat the air
until it came out clean. The gutters could not contain
the steady grief of rain. She closed herself up tight
like a house she planned to leave.

When she loved us again, we thought it was a trick
of the light. Her hands steadied. She sang
to the roosting hens. She gave us heels of bread
for the sparrows. She bought a summer dress
and seasoned a new black skillet. She filled the hollow
of her empty bed with a curl of napping boys.
She dreamed of trilling frogs. She waved again at trains.

AMY CRANE JOHNSON

Palm Springs for the First Time

from July/August 2004

Here, where desert palms offer praise
to gods I've never felt
before,
landlocked oregano heat
blisters the tongue and lizards
melt into sand and stone.
Here, where movement is
slow,
left to my own devices,
I just might go
feral,
spread myself eagle, like the one overhead,
set loose a coyote howl,
let dry wind chap inner
thighs, open wide to a world
not possible
in waves of laundry,
paperwork,
SUVs,
DVDs,
heavy metal,
PCPs, pumped-up, jumped-up
hipsters and gangsters,
MTV and wannabes.

Here, in full blaze,
ripe as a prickly pear blossom,
I just might become one
with a high-noon shadow,
sink in a desert wave,
erase my watered-down world,
sleep in the palm
of a newfound god.

KENNETH POBO

Fur Breakfast

from April/May 2015

Art Object by Meret Oppenheim

To gain the friendship of objects,
I beg the vacuum cleaner to swallow me whole.
                    I'm dangerous

around a cranberry red candy dish.
The furry cup and saucer shame me.
I become both coffee and sugar,

fingers touching the handle.
The cup stretches in a spot of sunlight,
  ripples the sip.

GRZEGORZ WRÓBLEWSKI

Important Message

from July/August 2006

Translated from the Polish by the author and Joel Leonard Katz

Walking in the forest
I met a friend who died
a few years ago. Patiently, he followed me
and when I rested... he too

sat on an adjacent stump. He said nothing
and I asked him nothing. We looked
into each other's eyes. Just like before. Later
I returned to town and turned in.

That night I saw him again.
I dreamt we were in the same
forest. And as earlier I asked him
nothing. He too said nothing.

ADITI MACHADO

The Photographer's Escape

from April/May 2009

The car is stuck mid-forest.
Leaves press against the face of my window,
the windshield, like the small palms of street children
at a red light. What do they want

so close to me where I can see the blood string
in their eyes, reticulate? I reach out, snap
the slender jugulars of creepers that hold tight
to the rearview mirror; slowly, edge
into the parking space of a great riverbank.

I have survived. Little can be said of my camera:
it has confused itself with prey, its eye wary
of the slightest animal breath, the smell of fish bones;
it looks small, even on a tripod,
as if poised on a skyscraper, about to jump.

MARK MAGOON

From the Fire

from July/August 2014

There is firework show in Wakefield
in the backyard on the Fourth of July

amongst the legs of my parents. It takes place
the year I burnt the soles of my shoes,

melted them on the grate of the fire.
That night and each one after, every girl

wears a tiny t-shirt and bouncy hair. That night
I snuck beers from my parents' party,

poured out a bit of cola
and poured some whiskey in

to drink as much as they were. Now
there's nothing but movement behind trees.

Everything blurs in drunken eyes and
goes onward, the night gets darker.

I remember orange faces in the glow.
I almost remember the way home.

I remember the first explosions
from the Black Cats I put into the flames—

the little red stars that fell
the sky. And the heads

as everyone leaned in and squinted,
waiting to see how bright it would get.

BRAD BOSTIAN

Land's End

from August 1997

In that dream of not belonging,
I take the sand-spurs and the heel-burning road
Down to the land's end to make my reacquaintance
With the tides, nodding on my way at fish in buckets,
And fishermen tideless as if they sat in great Sunday houses.
Sunburned, the sand cares nothing for me, the spray, the tides,
The currents too strong, the insects hiding in buzz and drone,
Glass and cans and fishing line, cigarette butts and one-legged
gulls;
And gray-green water. What if there were another way to baptize
ourselves,
Washing only for the sake of the body but letting the soul collect
its spurs?
The beauty of the sea comes out of the soulless pull below the
living soup,
Its mineral disregard for anything that swims or walks.
I love it because it doesn't care for me or any thing, I could kill
Every fish and the sea would keep washing itself dirty
And clean, dirty
And clean.

DOROTHEE LANG

Swallow

from October/November 2006

When you have the hiccups,
someone's thinking of you
somewhere in the world,
my grandma explained to me once

while I sat in her kitchen
on my embroidered cushion
counting the tapestry roses
that grew in rows on the wall.

Tell me about your school day,
she would always say,
and I would tell her about
the fossils of birds, the way they

can last forever when they fall
to the ground in the right place
and how they are made to plates
to hang on the auditorium wall.

When I arrived too late for lunch
she told me not to worry,
the youngest and the oldest
have a right to be heedless,

she would state, and leave
the door accidentally open.
But what if I want
the hiccups to stop,

I asked one day, there,
between strawberry jars.
Then you drown a sugar cube
in vinegar and swallow it,

she said, and I thought
it was a joke until I tried.
Until this sweet sour taste
blended into the memory of her.

KELLY NELSON

Depression

from April/May 2013

My Helen days
I call them

those days when I barely warm
my own skin, lift my own

limbs, when the barista
mishears, writes Helen on my cup,

the hard K of me
swallowed

as I'm lost
to the spiral

handed down from dark wintering drunks. The few people
I've told imagine I dread her

but I don't.
Helen shuffs off

illusion, sits in one place,
guards me better than I guard myself.

JILLIAN MERRIFIELD

Love and Sickness in the Time of ISIS

from January/February 2015

My boyfriend asks me what I think about the Dutch teens who went and joined the militants. They're pregnant and want to come home. I say there must have been something wrong in their lives long before they ran away to join the men with guns.

My father and I watch the news and see the young American woman who was going to join them through Tunisia and be a nurse and take up arms if necessary. She was intercepted by the FBI. He says it makes him think of his little sister, who met a man on the Internet, like she'd met so many men on the Internet before, and up and left her husband and her son and then up and left the country for Tunisia. This was before we cared about ISIS and after decades of medications and dangerous decisions. She was gone for a month and a half. I watched her vigilantly on Facebook, stalked her friends, tried to follow the chains of people into an understanding of how this could happen to a middle-aged woman from small-town Kansas, but she was quiet, and then she came home. We're sure she's on the lists that people keep, her name lurking in the hard drives of Homeland Security. People say we look alike. I've never seen it, which is perhaps an aggressive stance.

My aunt's not living at the farm anymore. Her mother and her ex-husband and her son live there, where she left them. I've heard that roofing nails occasionally appear scattered at the end of the gravel driveway, casual terrorism until you remember that people fly down that country road, ready to launch themselves and anybody else beyond.

ANTONIA CLARK

Chameleon Moon

from October/November 2009

On some fall days, you could smell the burning
everywhere. Backyard leaf piles, rubbish in rusted
metal drums, smoldering tires at Ratty's junkyard.

At night, smoke drifted over the roofs, seeped
into windows and dreams with news of bombed
cities, midnight arsonists, flames that licked slyly

along baseboards or leapt from kitchen cupboards.
Wind scurried ashes along the streets and gutters.
And the chameleon moon blinked its liquid eye.

We shivered in the heat, kicked free of the sheets
and pulled them up again. We turned to our lovers
and turned away at the touch of burning flesh.

C. S. BHAGYA

On rain

from October/November 2012

This is a poem about rain,
not you,
so you will forgive me
if I only refer to you in the oblique,
fleetingly,
between the L-shaped sounds
of water,
shadowy places,
and a cerise sky.
Sometimes,
when the night is deep,
you are out on the streets
and I'm waiting for sleep,
I send out rain
to follow you,
lopsidedly, as if a kind
ghost, as if through an
hourglass
you were seeing
sand at a slant.
So if I open the window a little,
swaying against glass,
test the air
for a possibility of rain,

perhaps you will forget
how, sometimes,
rain is complicated,
rain can break you if it wants.
Who knew, one night
rain under streetlamps
would aspire to the condition
of glow-worms?
This rain is a letter,
how it pulses through,
angling words
out of the slow scent of raw earth,
sudden lights.
But this poem is rain,
on you.

MARJORIE MIR

Sunlight and Shadow, 1884, William Merritt Chase

from April/May 2015

I

At a table under sycamores,
he lingers over coffee.
Young, lightly mustached,
in an ice-cream suit and spats,
he is looking past his tilted cup
toward a woman in a hammock,
asleep, or nearly so.
She lies withdrawn
within its curve,
one hand curled against her face,
black-stockinged ankles crossed.
The pale-rose fabric of her dress
drapes the hammock's side.

Before she left her chair to rest,
they drank, ate bread,
spooned honey from a patterned jar.
He smoked, glanced at the paper
now half-folded at his feet.
Not much was said, or had to be.

The air smells of his smoke,
coffee, honey, trees' leaves and bark.
Damp flower scents drift over
from the neighbor's yard
where an older woman bends,
back toward us,
watering her plants.

Sounds? The clink of his cup
against the saucer's edge,
the hammock's creak,
water splashing in the yard next door.
From the street,
a child's game, call-and-answer,
the rattling approach and fade
of iron wheels on stone,
sounds distant, intermittent.
It is Sunday, summer, quiet here.

•

II

Look beyond the quiet scene,
late morning, breakfast out-of-doors,
and see, just near its close,
a Henry James novella:
the young man in his linen suit
a painter
not long returned from Europe
to New York,

the woman in the hammock
an early love, first subject.
At twenty-six, the Jamesian spinster,
she teaches music
in her small front room;
in the years apart from him,
composed a life of work and friends.

Unsure, since his return,
of heart or home,
he has, this Sunday morning,
made his choice.

She is not, as it appears, asleep
but in retreat, regathering herself
and will, when he is gone,
collect the cups and rinse them,
put away the bread,
move back into her days' good grace.
By summer's end, or sooner,
that meeting-place of trees and sun,
the arc between those sycamores
will be her own again.

JUDE GOODWIN

Her Music

from January/February 2012

I spend a portion
of each day in the music
of our child. She rushes home,
drops coat and books
on the table, before
her snacks, before her laptop,
she pulls the bench out,
a loyal friend
waiting waiting worn
and wobbly
for her return,
she pulls the bench out
and sits, touches the piano keys
only lightly
then presses her young soul
into their arms
and dances there—
a waltz at first,
then sonata to the garden,
sonatina for the little dog—
dances and the air lights up,
a hundred cascading points of song.
If I stand behind her
they move over my body,

up my back, when I breathe
they fill my lungs.
I close my eyes
and the sun is rising,
or appearing suddenly
from behind a storm cloud,
the room is filled
with god rays,
or there's a dark rose bud
blooming in a tall glass vase,
growing rounder then folding
over, dropping its petals
to the polished wood,
or there's a girl,
slender armed,
bent over such fierce fingers
a dozen young men
holding black and white horses
call out to her
Away. Away.

MARGARET HOLLEY

I See My Long Dead Mother in the Shop 'n Save

from October/November 2015

Fifty years gone, and yet here she is,
exactly her profile, every wave and curl
in place, navy cardigan over her trim figure,

sleeves pushed up to the elbows as usual,
a plastic bag dangling from her fingers,
as she leaves the checkout lane and pauses

to chat with two other women,
every cell in me quivers on high alert,
my breath leaps headlong over the barricade

of Vidalia onions and brown baking potatoes,
the prison of fresh produce, a teenage
soul scrambles easily over Himalayas

of decades and frozen finalities,
teeters on the edge of two worlds till
I'm clear out of my mind for five seconds

of pure joy, thin wedge of a scream
muted by speechless amazement to see her
here, just looking young and happy,

when suddenly she laughs, turns toward
the heavy Exit door, and walks out
into the sunshine of mortal day.

JOHN GREY

The Long Drive

from October/November 2012

Flat Midwestern road,
towns sleeping even in the daylight,
farmhouses, though, bustling early,
men in faded blue overalls,
women in old print dresses
on the front steps shouting something,
kids darting back and forth between the two;
white wooden church, linseed mill,
a flock of grackles descending on a crop,
cows, haystacks, fences long and lean
as the train-lines running parallel;
look ahead and I can see as far as the next silo
and the next and the next;
look behind and...
no, there's no looking behind;
radio playing, FM country, AM talk,
singing to myself,
laughing at the sheer humbuggery of the callers;
don't bother the speedometer with a glance,
car's like an airplane,
faster we travel, the more we're standing still;
van ahead of me
pulling off into a side road,
almost got to where he's going...
so it can be done, I tell myself.

LUCAS JACOB

Declaring Victory

from January/February 2014

Thirteen times I went to the edge
of the water. Once a day for
nearly two weeks. The white birds stood
indifferent to my comings
and unaware of my goings.
Once I took a photo of a
sunflower on the bank, not knowing
of a field of them just downstream.

Had I known, I might have gone so
far as to try to find a way
to snap one of the stalks down low
enough to obscure the fact of
the theft, the flower field being
hard against a one-strand wire fence.
As it was, I let the photo
be the stem and blooming of my

wish. That I would stay true to this
new resolve. That the river run
high enough to move the egrets
onto larger stones. That the one
in thought give way to the two in
words. In a field of words, their sound
a rush like wind past thick stalks, like
the flappings of wings uncounted.

MARY MERIAM

Facts about Romance

from October/November 2009

The neighbor's cat is here again.
A heron bombs the silver blooms.
Moonrise lights the soggy tombs.
I go to sleep, wake up, and then,
who can tell me why or when,
creeping by the witchy brooms,
the neighbor's cat is here again.
A heron bombs the silver blooms.
Swear and sign it with a pen!
Follow her, the verdict looms.
Rush her from the rising rooms,
the bed of lavender, the wren.
The neighbor's cat is here again.

JUDY KABER

If I hadn't picked up the turkey feather

from January/February 2015

it might still be lying on the ground,
slightly mangled now by rain, by wind,
by the peculiarity of dirt's domain.

I might still be staring at a passing car,
caught in the thick craw of going or
not going, harpooned to the moment,

forgetting to look down, to caress
the careless treasures found in the garden
by the roadside, the gravelly seeds

of the fallen, the abandoned, the dispossessed.
I might be humming a lullaby, my arms
empty as the turkey footprints depressed

in mud. I might have forgotten the way
home, the rich drape of sympathy roosting
in my bed, the beauty of loss.

JULIE KING

Willing

from April/May 2001

You are thirteen and pregnant
and don't know who the father

is but do know he doesn't want
to know. You think about peaches

on the windowsill and their velvet
skin and how it wouldn't hurt

if you bit into one right now,
before they are ready. You wish

for the Fourth of July carnival
when you rode and rode the ferris

wheel and when you reached up
your arms, the air pushed your palms

in a friendly way. You wonder
how much of this matters and if it

doesn't, why do you want to run
down the middle of the street

yelling *fire* to the junkyard dogs
free in their yards or anyone else

who will tear out your throat?

(Poem selected for inclusion by Jennifer Finstrom)

CAROLYN STICE

Mama at thirty

from January/February 2014

After Edward Hirsch

Halfway between birth and now she drove east
put fifteen hundred miles between us, and my father
moved us into a shabby white

house with an empty kitchen, a basement, full of rats.
We heard them in the night, their scrapping
and squeaks, while Mama worked downtown

hustling her tables on the night shift. She and my sister
battled daily over nothing it seemed
and afterward my sister would slam our bedroom door

blasting music to drown my cries. I'd crawl in bed
with Mama, and she would curl her body around
my toddler self, hand on my stomach, her words

be still now humming in my ears.
She was thirty and I was two. Now I have slipped, into her
skin as my daughter calls in the night, saying *cuddle me*

and I wrap my limbs, around hers, pull
her close until her chest is tucked, against mine.
Some days there is space for nothing else but this:

the mother in me alone, with her child in the dark.
This is a space too small for fathers, or the slam
of doors echoing, through a windy old house.

There is only the deepening of our bodies
into breath, and the slackening
of the cord between us that has grown

ever more taut as our separate lives
pull us apart. Tonight the wind
whispers and the cicadas hum, the trees vibrate

with the terrible and beautiful weight of generations
and I can feel the dark sky heavy above the house
pregnant with rain, coming down on us all.

ELLEN KOMBIYIL

When the Rivers Were Still Clean, the Old Men Said Take Her Down and Save Her

from July/August 2006

You're going to Hell and your mother is, too,
her grandmother told her. So one Sunday
she wore her white Polly Flanders
with the smocking on front and loose bow
of baby bloom satin at the waist.

For someone so steeped in sin,
she expected a full soaking, robed
singers, special lighting, a feeling
of lifting, but it was just a sprinkle
transferred from his fingers to the crown
of her head. Later, in another
summer, she would recall the sensation:
standing under porch eaves in a dressing
gown too thin for the weather, syncopatic
plitt, platt, and lips still wet from kissing,
she waited for the rain to ease before
dashing up the front steps into the house.

JENNIFER FINSTROM

Las Vegas

from April/May 2013

My ex-husband grew up there, and I think again
of the stories he told me as I pack a small
bag and prepare to travel west for a conference.
I had myself grown up near Milwaukee, another
planet, so when he told me of how all of his neighbors'
yards were braceletted by high walls, dogs snarling
on their other sides, how his garage was nested
full of black widow spiders, how people checked
their shoes for the tiny scorpions that might
be hidden there, I turned my own shoes upside
down even living in Madison, as if he might
have brought those small and poisonous creatures
with him. He told me how he and his friend
would go out into the desert when they were boys,
where it is now identical house after identical
house, and catch snakes and lizards in a bucket,
sneaking them home, and how one day,
they saw a small sidewinder making its way
in fluid curves across the blowing sand.
They dumped their bucket without a word,
scattering what they had gathered, the various
skinks and whiptails, around their feet. The side-
winder was young, and they caught it easily, arguing
over who would be the one to slide the cover

under the vault of the bucket's opening. I don't
remember who finally did it, but the snake lived
for many years in a closet aquarium, kept a secret
from both of their mothers, fed on white mice
and crickets, its water dish filled as soon
as it emptied, its slither useless out of the sand.

(Poem selected for inclusion by Julie King)

ROBERT OKAJI

Memorial Day

from July/August 2014

Arriving at this point
without knowledge of the journey,

the slow collapse and internal
dampening—the shutting down, the closing in—lost

in the shadowed veil, my eyes flutter open to find
everything in its place, yet

altered, as if viewed from a single step
closer at a different height, offering a disturbing

clarity. Looking up, I wonder that she wakes me
from a dream of dogs on this, of all days,

only to detect under me linoleum in place of the bed,
my glasses skewed from the impact,

the floor and left side of my head wet. You looked
like you were reaching for something, she says,

and perhaps I was, though with hand outstretched
I found nothing to hold but the darkness.

KATHLEEN KIRK

Juncos

from April/May 2011

In winter, invisible on the leaf-layered, snow-dusted lawn,
slate-colored juncos, dozens at a time.

Mud birds I call them, after the dark gray
mud birds I gave to my mother one Christmas,

captured in rough clay. My mother
loves them as I do, for their modest, persistent

beauty. She sets them out on the dark wood table
where they hide. She glues back a broken beak.

In winter, they are always among us, seed-seeking,
silent, gorgeous in their gray.

MIRIAM KOTZIN

Albino

from January/February 2012

The deer are on the move. I watch for them
while standing at the kitchen sink, my aunt's
white china sudsy in my hands. It's ten
o'clock, and I've a project to advance.

An albino buck's
in the neighborhood.
I'll lure him to my apple tree,
offer a sweet salt lick.

I'll make him come to me though all the earth's
white fog's been turned to flesh in him. I heard
the gunshots echo from the woods today.
The deer are on the move. I watch for them.

COURTNEY GUSTAFSON

Grief Reaction

from July/August 2015

When she was at her sickest, small
and yellow, my mother appeared pregnant
in my dreams, healthy and glowing,
with the bad perm she had in her thirties.
She had been trying for a long time, I think.

When the baby was born
it was made out of paper.
My dad wore hospital scrubs and
he held it like he might rip it in half,
this white origami infant,
and my mom looked at him eagerly,
waiting to hear that it had all ten
fingers and toes.

They left the baby in a recycling bin
on the way out of the hospital.
Everything was dark. When I woke up
I remembered that my mom was dying.
And this might be the best thing
I can do for her: to let her be
the one who is dying.

RANJANI MURALI

Drug Dogs

from April/May 2015

When you land in this foreign city, where a closed-circuit
camera projects your grainy face into rooms full of strudels
and steaming tea, the taste of metal in the air and baggage
reeking of rain and spring-weeds catches your throat.

You were afraid of dogs since the day a stray
chased you (then a six-year-old eating a tomato
sandwich on your way to abacus classes), squeezing
the sound of pumping blood into your teeth,

wrenching the acid from your stomach, spraying
it into a pool of vomit in the bushes nearby.
Now, the muscled black figures follow your
bags, taking in their scent, the way your fingertips

quiver in the tubelights, your sweaty hair. When an officer
pats you on the back, you turn around, and the sandwich
you are clutching in your hand materializes out of
a meek memory, ready to be torn at, and ready to be

released, half-masticated onto these floors, where
the dogs sniff at you again, and again.

SHARON McDERMOTT

Crows: The Yard

from April/May 2010

Here's the digestible map: tracks of the great
black birds in the snow. You have fed the monks

of the winter trees shelled nuts, sunflower
seed, suet, and they've gone off to pray. The world

blizzards by, whitens like the knuckles of a fearful
hand. You have fed the black-coated warriors

grapes, dried berries, bits of days-old bread, and they
have gone off to battle. February carves itself

ice sculpture. Great clouds of crows eclipse
the falcon's own lonely hunger, which cries out

like a high wind: *shree! shree!* The map is a trudged
field, the snow fills footsteps behind you. You fed

the thieving humps, cloaked and hunkered down
in oaks and elms. You fed them all, driven simply

by their hunger, and they circled like a great smoke
ring. Here's the digestible map: the cold world brings

out need, eyes that pierce like stars. You learn to feed
what cannot feed itself, the catcalling monks, the cassocked

friars. Call down the great black fire—trees will feather
into wings and move closer: the answered prayer, nearing.

BOB BRADSHAW

Digging up a 19th Century Steamboat

from July/August 2008

My brother was an amateur psychic
who drank too much
and had no direction in his life.

He swore there was a steamboat
buried under our feet.
He swore that if we found it,
he'd give up drinking.

What could I do? I sank a shovel
into our celery field,
and I began to dig.

From the width of an archery target,
our hole soon gaped like a cistern.
Then crumbling cliffs.
We could have been digging
our way across Panama,

the way landslides oozing
from slopes rafted down on us,
determined to keep their secrets.

Water squirmed upwards
from old springs.
Pumps were brought in.
A paddlewheel emerged from the slop.

Clothes, tobacco pipes, the steamer's second deck
began to rise like a man
long buried in a peat bog.

Spoons, agates, dolls, and broken axles surfaced
the way that Roman coins and nails
have worked their way up to ground level

across the fields of Europe.
What had we uncovered?

What we'd found was something
we had always known, but so disturbing
that we had always passed over it:

that like this steamer, our lives
were merely passing

through.

JACK MURPHY

Bikes

from July/August 2015

At 13 and filled with whatever is it that makes 13-year-olds go,
bored and restless, in love with our joints and muscles, in love
with the feeling of pedals churning and ping of hollow aluminum bats
connecting with baseballs, with metal poles, chain link fences,
old broken pop machines, with anything that stood out, and
had having spent another afternoon of our last summer running
and swimming and fighting and swearing, sun-bronzed
above the neck and beneath the elbows and below the
knees, how disappointed we were, how truly dejected, to
emerge from the house to find our bikes still sprawled
on the lawn by my mother's azaleas, right where we'd left them,
to find they had in fact not been stolen by the neighbor kids
from the middle school. What loss it was to slink back into the dark
air conditioning of the concrete basement without a score to settle,
an injustice to correct, a battle to wage, a dream to labor for.

ELIZABETH KERPER

Using Azalea as a Verb

from July/August 2015

Its meaning would begin with our grandfather,
though not because of the gardens he tended
all the years of our growing up. To azalea
would not mean to prop up the long neck
of the apple tree, grown too heavy with sour
fruit to raise its head, nor to shoulder the roll
of bubble wrap and mend the cold frames
torn after another winter, not even to raise
a whole tomato in both hands to your mouth
and bite, though we can remember our grandfather
doing all of those things. Verbing azalea

would have more to do with the basement of his house,
the orange concrete floor pocked with hollows
and divots, the open buckets of loamy dirt
he mixed with sand and sterilized by the panful
in the oven, the soil as much a product of his labor
as anything that bloomed from it—the soil
and the serrated knives with blades the length
of our arms he used to keep it from settling,
those knives studding each bucket
and no one telling us not to touch them.

Or maybe it would mean playing
our basement games, we sisters and cousins
becoming orphans and runaways,
whole worlds imagined with all the grownups evil
or vanished. This was when our uncle still lived
in the basement bedroom, stacking cans of Skoal
like quarters on the dresser; this was when our mothers
thought that would be the thing that killed him,
so we did too. To azalea: to tempt loss,
then reascend to the kitchen, windows open,
green peppers and ears of corn on the counter,
our grandmother dozing in her chair.

TARA WYNNE

Bare Metal

from April/May 2003

Behind the garage, chrome crumples from the sun's stiff beating,
bunches in on itself until it looks like a giant mouth lost all
its fillings there, where the bumpers and grilles had once been.
Those cars back there are all partscars. My favorite one
is the grey goose, a Starliner that *got it* when a tree dropped a branch,
heavy as a thigh, through the Ford's windshield.

That happened back when we never had *the money*,
when Dad was a clerk at Whitlock Auto Parts in Racine.
When Mom would take me shopping to Zaires for schooldress
fabric, or bathtub bleach, or mousetraps, we'd stop over by Dad
and I'd wander the air freshener aisle, fingering the trees
until my hands smelled like fruit cocktail.

My dad had a nametag—KENNETH—even though Mom and most
others have always called him *Kenny* or *Junior*. After he quit
because they were telling him what to do, he never got another job.
He began to work on cars at home, since then has smelled like bondo
and paint thinner, and now people can call him whatever they want.

The partscars slowly sag, their rusted bellies settling
into the grass. Meanwhile, mice take over under their hoods,
moss furs over the benchseats, our pets climb or jump
through open windows and sleep inside. I can tell when our girldog,
Molly, has been curled inside one—her nose and eyelashes
are glittered with whatever the dust of a dying car is called.

The partscars have all shed their paintjobs. Even though Dad paints
hundreds of cars, always puts the clearcoat on tight,
I know they'll all fail, once they give in to the Wisconsin wintersalt.
Once, at the junkyard, Dad found a car he'd painted. I was waiting
in the truck, Molly panting behind me, and through the windshield
I watched Dad's face go like a sodacan under a bootheel.

Mom wishes Dad would wear his facemask when he's painting.
She laughs sometimes, *Your father must have garagedust and paint
on the inside of his lungs*. What color are they now? Before winter
got there, I bet they looked like trinkets, mirroring a million colors
against the plumred sun of his heart. He thinks they'll be safe there,
but he doesn't know better, doesn't know his heart pumps rust.

POOJA GARG SINGH

Stroke

from October/November 2014

You were in ICU. I was cutting ladyfingers
on my chopping board, slicing them lengthwise

removing their heads exactly 7,955 miles away. I know
I see it on Google maps everyday. There you are—

An octagon marked by a blue arrow, which I imagine
digging deep into your room, into your TV blaring blue

Today it was silent when I called you
You were silent too. You were sleeping I was told

You slept like that for ten more days
My phone did not wake you up

When it finally did, on eleventh day
I heard your voice like water

pushing its way over jagged stones
Crackling like a telephone connection gone bad

A connection I am still trying to restore
after ninety-eight days, after being told I need to hurry

BARBARA DE FRANCESCHI

Christmas on a Sheep Station

from October/November 2006

there is nothing subtle
about plucking a wild duck
turquoise head limp
against a soft brown chest / voice box silent

I am twelve years old
whisked from urban to rural Australia
where commodities are precious
conservation respected in every crude form

black leeches stick to my legs
after a swim in the creek
ghostly flutes piped through red-gum stands
sigh in sympathy
as I apply common salt to save my blood

I learn to squirt milk into a bucket
from a cow's bulging teat
fill vacola jars with fruit
grown in an orchard
that survives on bore water and chicken shit

in solid darkness with a narrow torch beam
I navigate the pathway to the lavatory
avoid being bitten by furry black tweezers
or spooked by the vaporous bleat
of a stray lamb

but I cannot tear feathers
from a dead chestnut teal

around a Christmas table
set with no nonsense
fragile bones rise on white china plates
for me... sweet potato and sticky dumplings

L.I. HENLEY

Cancer

from January/February 2010

The familiar small-knuckled tap on my front door,
our landlady who shares the duplex
who's got two fat eggplants, one in each hand,
and says, "He's sick," and at first I think she means
her dog, Goose, who gets nervous and pukes,
and I wonder why he'd want to eat eggplant anyways.
And then I remember: *Melanzane alla Parmigiana* for her
boyfriend whom I've never met, who lives alone
like she lives alone. She makes him pizza
every Thursday, has done so for years, and tonight
they were going to try something new, spice up
their routine with a new dish.
She is my mother's age, in the middle
of her life like a rowboat at sea,
always reading when she eats
and sometimes sitting on her side of the fence
doing pastel drawings of the redwoods,
blackberry bushes, and cypress.
Her boyfriend is dying.
I know almost every day she must hear
Jonathan and I having sex
and laughing and dancing around
like the first couple in the garden,
heathens, eating and fucking and spilling Charles Shaw
on the rented blue carpet. We try to be quiet.

But our crockery is always boiling over and rarely
do we think of the dark behind the darkness.
I stand with the door open even when she's gone,
even when the cold is coming in, uninvited,
and settling down on everything we own,
even when the snow blows in
and we begin to freeze into statues of our young, hard selves.

GARY DOP

Iowa Summer

from July/August 2014

Before meth's magic collapsed
your face, before you pimped
your girlfriend to pay for gas

and grass on your joyride
to Vegas, we mowed lawns
in Indianola to buy chips and

cherry cola from the corner sundry
and that styrofoam airplane
to soar over the playground.

We hid behind the plastic
jungle, ate our Cool
Ranch Doritos, and with our toes

disappearing in sand, we stared
high above ourselves, wondering why
the wings blew off

and the whole thing turned
from the open sky and missiled
to the breaking ground.

ARJUN RAJENDRAN

pyre

from pril/May 2012

we were on the playground
when smoke from the pyre billowed above our heads

we tried stoning the sky,
to see if we could hit a skull behind all that dark energy

birds crashed into these pillars
of truth, as if the rest of their flight were mere illusion

we stood in awe watching
the wind eat every morsel, lick its fingers clean in the dusk

and all that was left of the pyre
by morning was a trapezoid of ash and buffalo piss

NICOLE BORG

Talking to the Dead

from April/May 2012

Someone has been trying to
send me a message for
weeks—my car keys missing,
pyramids of coins stacked neatly
in corners, lamps turned on I
know I've shut off, toast crumbs on
the counter making the profile of a face.

The scuttling in the attic does
not sound animal—when I climb up
there's old insulation, inches
of dust and this heaviness
I can't shake.

If I could mail one letter to
the dead, it would be a chain
letter—*Send this to the ten*
people you loved the most—
to see if it returned to me.

DAVID MATHEWS

Where Did That Come From?

from January/February 2014

I remember sitting there,
staring at my shoes, which seemed
to be as big as a clown's,
while my stepdad was telling
a sliding scale shrink
how he knew I was just a kid,
but he couldn't help but hate
everything about me.

I don't remember what the shrink
said in response to my own
personal Grendel
who like his namesake,
struck usually after drinking,
when everyone else was asleep.

That mental portrait just popped
right into my head from nowhere,
while at a stoplight,
going home from a bad day at work.
Was that the trigger?
Or has it just been slowly
fighting its way back
to the center stage of my mind,
ever since I forgot?

JENNIFER FINSTROM

The Only Memory I Have of Being Thin

from January/February 2000

For two days about ten years ago,
I was thinner than I have ever been.
I was barely alive.
The world could not contain me.

It was summer and my room
was hot. I napped, and between
napping, read. I can picture
the book beside me, a paperback

copy of *Anna Karenina*. The woman
on its cover was corseted and
shapely. She was wearing
a black dress decorated with lace

and looking over her shoulder.
My awareness rose and fell
like an underwater face. Sometimes
I knew that I was lying

flat and limp, but sometimes
I was standing in a crowd.
I carried a small red purse,
its strap wrapped twice

around my hand. Soon
I would be the first to see
what shook the ground and roared,
the hungry demon hooked

by the lodestar of my heart.

(Poem selected for inclusion by Tom Dooley)

JESSY RANDALL

Snow White Sick

from January/February 2000

I have been hysterically poisoned
Snow White not wanting the prince

I lie on my glass mattress
my head made of glass, and my body

shrinking, pale, a thin white moon
in the blue dark of the forest

poetry is not a cure; it cannot
be bled from me, swallowed pink

angrily fighting the source
of this illness. Somewhere

in this building is clear, clear
water for me to drink

SHANNON CONNOR WINWARD

Paracusia

from January/February 2013

1.

Sometimes voices wake me from my dreams
and follow me throughout the day

déjà vu
a record, skipping.

Considered alone
their conversation is innocuous

Libraries are westerly.
Throw out the chicken.

but as a lingual bridge
from dream to reality

iloveyouiloveyou
wait!

I can't shake the notion
that I should wake up

and pay attention.

2.

I drew my bedspread
across a burning candle
and caught the edge on fire.

As I tried to put it out
an old woman stood over my shoulder
insisting I was doing it wrong

so I began to blow
great, desperate puffs of air
but the flames engulfed the bed.

        For Godssake,
she shouted.
        Stop breathing.

3.

Sometimes I wake up gasping.

4.

Our bedroom was brighter when I woke
than it was when I fell asleep.

I searched every room.
I checked the ashtray.

I collapsed beside my husband
but struggled against sleep

convinced that if I drifted off
the fire would become real

the place would fill with smoke
and I would die

curled around his body in a rigid *S*
as he snored and dreamed of things

that stay where they belong.

RK BISWAS

Broken Chimes

from July/August 2014

A jeering breeze, flying in from the west,
has taken down my wind chimes
one by one. Each string
twisted, turned, snapped like a wishbone.
The pieces flying to the ground.
Falling
flat like dead birds.

Last week the breeze took two.
Shooting them
down with shrill cries. Today
it took one. And is already
eyeing another. The last one standing
is made of brass.
Linked together like festive lights.

They say a chain is as strong
as its weakest link.
But why me? What does he want?
I have done nothing
to get in the way. I have in fact
bent over backwards to give.
And yet I am betrayed.

MARC FRAZIER

November, 2013

from January/February 2015

The doe approaches slowly,
driven by this season's early freeze,

nibbles at frozen kale, seedpods,
jerks her head up at any hint of sound,

dangerously close to the house.
We marvel at her vigilance,

the weight of staying alert,
every moment vulnerable.

"How like us," I want to say but don't
because we seldom say what matters.

What to do with this empty seat
where you should be this time of year?

Near the end you asked me, "Am I dying?"
The nurse upped the morphine

and your rattle calmed.
I was already writing your obit,

awash in the distance of third person
to speak of the first person in my life.

The deer disappears into the woods.
A late autumn sun sets on white Wisconsin hills.

All the way home I recall these lines:
The language of loss does not travel back,

is endless, and speaks too tenderly
from no one to no one.

Italicized lines from David Rigsbee's poem, "When We All Split Up"

PATRICIA L. JOHNSON

On the North Shore

from October/November 2014

At first the bird appeared a migrating Goldfinch,
odd for early October in Louisiana. The warbler's
breast shone bright, downy and rounded. I studied
the bird through binoculars from a breath away.

The last verified sighting of a Bachman's occurred
in Cuba decades ago. Believed extinct, some trust
the warbler survives beyond human reach. One
ornithologist claims it's impossible to spot.
"People will not believe you. They'll call it Bigfoot."
Yet he instructs, "get a picture if the bird returns."
A whole summer and a fall the warbler stayed away.

Warbler species feed in various ways. My warbler
hopped as she fed, nudging pine needles, eating the insects
that spilled to the ground. She was a mature bird,
accomplished in each move. Her breast equal to Audubon's
drawing—olive blending to cream-yellow. Her beak
perfected for its purpose, a gentle, decurved bill.

The Eastern guidebook states Bachman's Warblers
inhabit hidden swamps, like the bayou one mile away—
forbidden, unfathomable—yet I would set foot there
for a truer glimpse. I caught my warbler on film
when she returned one evening, sent the video
to the museum though it was grainy. The ornithologist
dubbed it a common yellowthroat; although
long ago I eliminated that ordinary bird.

GRETA BOLGER

Reverberations

from October/November 2008

From deep in the leafy ravine behind
the barn, the blast was barely audible.

Shotgun to mouth, forked limb stuck in dirt
to serve as the extra hand none of us

would have lent to this catastrophe.
Why must children kill themselves this way,

demand our belated attention with bits
of precious flesh the dog brings home days later?

Unbelieving, we delve into dark speculation:
was it wishes not granted, permissions withheld?

Imperfect loving rewound first reel to last,
the final frames always the same.

Cats howl, darkness gathers, young mourners
huddle on patchy grass, sneaking cigarettes.

The priest rearranges his toolbox, neighbors boil
eggs and slice ham, florists stick stems in green foam.

The machinery of grief-tending slips into gear
while numb and blind as a blindfolded bat,

a mother unwilling to go on
goes on, riddled, leafless, undone.

ASEEM KAUL

Invisible Man

From October/November 2010

Not invisible but transparent:
his presence betrayed
by the glint of the occasional edge
or the small dislocation
his body made passing through
the light: a shift in awareness,
a silence magnified.

The way sometimes, at sunset,
his heart would break
the last ray of the sun, splitting
the blue from the crimson,
staining the dusk with its mood.

After the first crack we knew
it was a matter of time,
the veins of the fault
growing like cancer, flaw
joined to flaw to make
a cobweb of pain—

he hung on a long while—

but shattered, in the end,
into a thousand pieces
so small that even now
I will find one in a corner
gleaming quiet as a star.

RAY TEMPLETON

Visitors

From April/May 2014

These days, you know more of the dead—
ones you loved now rubbing shoulders

with old friends, colleagues, that man
you used to see at the market. It's fine—

and when they come
you're just a little more prepared:

the back of a head on the train,
a familiar kind of laugh—or something

that surprises, like the way light scatters
in ribbons across a lake in the wind,

a sudden scent of crushed angelica,
or a sense of movement in the dark

outside your kitchen door. But not
at your command—a question

to be asked, a face you feel the need to see,
displaced by the slight push of others

crowding, more from year to year. They're
there, wherever "there" might be: as the space

where light from one room illuminates another
and for a moment you see more clearly than ever.

CHRISTINE POTTER

Unforgetting

from April/May 2015

I think of my mother when I write fiction,
how she lost the way Chopin and Bach laid
their hands over hers while she practiced piano
like the kind uncles they weren't, how she lost

New York City's pure grey sky outside
her desk's 16th floor window at Macmillan,
lost even her squat, stop-sign-red Correcting
Selectric typewriter. I think of how she

remembers what she cannot remember.
The stories flood away from her but still
she scoops them to her lips and tells them.
This shouty new hamburger joint must

be the place where she went dancing after
the War. And didn't I love Spotty the terrier,
who nipped at the grocer's delivery boy
twenty years before I was born? I can't

say no. There's a Juliet balcony in Verona,
a Headless Horseman bridge in Sleepy Hollow.
And at Winchester Cathedral, a dazzling
maze of stained glass smashed to bits by

Cromwell, but leaded back together in
the Restoration—kings' heads, the hands
of saints, all out of context and bright as
anything broken, beautiful and gathering light.

ROHAN CHHETRI

A Difficult Mountain

From January/February 2011

A few days ago, since I had just received a paycheck,
I had offered to fund my mother's trip to the city.
Yesterday when I told her about the theft, we decided
to cancel the trip for now. She wasn't surprised.
She told me how every little grace that comes her way
is leveled by fate, how she keeps coming back,
razed right down to where she started from.
Years of defeat have taught her humility.
Like my discomfiture at the thought that the thieves
looked right into my sleeping eyes and left is
almost a feeling of violation. She tells me, these days
her dreams are of climbing uphill on a difficult mountain
where she is always falling short of footholds, or of climbing
an endlessly long flight of stairs. And if she gets to the top
somehow, she realizes there is no way back down.
I try to tell her it should be fine. Half-pleased that
she connects the metaphors, and half-scared she will
understand their immensities suddenly one day.

DAVID OESTREICH

Muse, Incognito

from April/May 2009

You will not find Epiphany
among the trees. The maples,
lifting bony fingers to the sky,
make no revelation; their
black eyes are blank, the dark
scrolls of their hearts, empty.
The wind's voice runs like a skink
through the leaves, upon
the bluff face, unintelligible
as the lichen hieroglyphs which
mark each stone. The moss
is wool, pulled down tight.
Others have sought her here;
their manic laughter echoes
in the woodcock's call. Still,
she will come, now, in this
moment between breaths,
but in no vision, with no voice
beside your own.

RUTH D. HANDEL

No Border Is Perennial

from April/May 2014

From a tangle of alien bushes a cane
of rambler rose. Blossoms elope.
Ragged. Pale pink.

No site for sentiment. Just the pulse
of sun-seeking blooms, thorns.
Always a surprise

for the seeing eye,
the chance flower or weed appearing
or not with its own particular insistence.

A moonflower seeded by wind
opens its petals, scents the evening.
Next season no trace.

Top-heavy peonies colonize
the curbside. Cargo of black ants
freeloading nectar.

Honeysuckle, stealth assassin, prepares
to wind its tendrils around
viburnum leaves.

Wild sweet william, black-eyed susan,
butterfly weed native to the place
grow without restraint

like crossbred thought no focus has contained.
What happens without plan finds order
in the welcome

of the eye whose gaze calls forth the lines.
Borders, against confusion
a momentary stay.

HIMALI SINGH SOIN

Invisible Poetry

from October/November 2014

Imagery like the piles of cauliflower stacked perfectly on the
trucks of Delhi.
Ellipses like the vanishing alleyways of Prague.
Semicolons like the gasp of the first sight of Baobabs in
Antananarivo.
Anonymous pronouns like the scones of London.
Margins like the white robes at Tiannamen Square.
Anaphora like the holes where the bombs fell in Berlin.
Metaphors like buds bursting through peeling walls in Lhasa.
Volta like when I met you in Paris.
Catalexis like leaving my shoes in Soussouvlei.
Rhyme like the man in penguin boxers and an orange tie on the
subway in Brooklyn.
Enjambment like the nomad that reached Ulan Bator.
Couplet like the orchid and the hummingbird in Cuzco.
Assonance like the popcorn drinkers of Addis, tone like
transcendentalism in Thimpu.
Sonnet like wandering and wondering, sonnet like all cities as
one.

LAINEY S. CRONK

Attic

from October/November 2013

One crow
beside a clean pebble path, as in a tidy painting,
turns her obsidian head, certainly symbolizing
something
that will lend itself to little lines of black ink
measured out across my narrow page—
but what, I've no idea,
light bulbs all unscrewed and lying aimlessly
about the attic, out of their protective sleeves,
and inspiration off in the Adirondacks with a recent lover,
spending a small tax refund and oblivious
to me, back home, walking the edge of an old black road
in dirty gray sneakers, passing a symbolic and lovely
crow which, at least for now, will have to be
nothing more than a large, dark bird.

CHIELOZONA EZE

Of Gods, Love, and Grandma

from October/November 2013

For my thirteenth birthday, a friend gave me
a mini-radio, silvery, glinting at every twirl.
I sat under an orange tree in front of our house,
listened to a story, laughed now and then.

My Grandma asked why I was amused.
Poseidon was the Greek god of the sea, I told.
Like other gods, he raped the maidens of Arcadia
the way he did to Medusa in Athena's temple.

Athena turned away from the evil, but punished
Medusa, changed her hair to revolting snakes.
Grandma did not turn away her face;
she merely asked: *Is that a reason to laugh?*

But that was years ago. Grandma is dead.
Many wars have been fought,
many more women and girls have been raped.
Leaves have yellowed, reddened, fallen.

Everything will pass away, I know,
but not Grandma's voice and brown eyes,
deep with many stories untold,
many questions yet to be answered.

RUTH BAUMANN

Small

from July/August 2012

The first & only time you were eight
you remember remembering being seven
& the religious fear that filled you
when you realized, growing up means
dying. Even worse than dying,
forgetting. If you were previously made of streamers,
now you alternated between thumbtacks &
gelatin. Around this time the sky birthed guilt
& it rained into your bones every day
sweet. *Good morning, thing I will carry the rest of my life,*
you should have said when the thing
that made you part of yourself, childhood-altering thing
all childhoods run temple-first into, first
smarted. But you didn't know any better
than to assume life was a series of events
that moved, that didn't get stuck on each other
& stretch forwards & backwards: but the brain
is a piece of taffy on a fork, the brain,
your brain, is a simple concoction of sugars & time,
& you are not always your brain.
The last & only time you were eight
you became nine.

ALEXANDRA SMYTH

Tyto Alba

from July/August 2012

I.

Tuesday morning my mother woke up to a murder of crows having a panic attack on the power lines that demarcate our front yard. She stepped out on to the porch, watching the crows fly back and forth, a neurotic symphony in darkness. The sun was just over the treetops when she finally realized the source of their anxiety. A barn owl sat on the hood of her champagne 1997 Ford Taurus. It turned its head imperceptibly until its eyes met her. The pupils overtook the iris. The eyes imperceptible black glass buttons. A thread of gaze connected them for a moment. My mother shuddered. A crow screeched. The owl took flight, up over the house, its wings spread as wide as my father's arms. The crows followed in restless pursuit.

II.

When I was sixteen I used to stay out too late on Saturday nights, making out with my Catholic school boyfriend in the backseat of my car. After dropping him off at his parents' house, I liked taking back roads to get to my own. Pulling onto Paul Spring Parkway one evening, I dropped my speed, a glint of fox eye night vision bumping off my headlights. It wasn't until after I went away to college that the city installed street lights on that section of the road. When I came to the stop sign at the intersection of Paul Spring Parkway and New Orleans Street, an owl swooped down and stood in the crosswalk. My headlights illuminated its eerily white face. It carried something in its round beak, a field mouse or a vole perhaps, too small for me to determine its genus and species. It tilted its head back and swallowed the creature in one elegant gulp. It tapped its left talon on the asphalt, then was gone.

SCOTT URBAN

Drought

from April/May 2013

Thunderheads peek over the horizon,
but—cruel teases—never drift any closer.

We watch The Weather Channel
as if we might hold the lotto's winning ticket.

A dozen raindrops
would be more welcome
than a tumbling Krugerrand.

The sky is so parched
it steals water from our pond.

What was once shore
is now baked clay shingles
that resemble the pattern on the back
of your grandmother's wrist.

Bluegill and catfish used to enjoy
the greenery where now we stand.

We wonder, *How much longer*
until there is no pond,
but only an oversized bowl
for the lowing, calf-heavy cow?

PAT SMITH

Jupiter

from July/August 2012

I see Jupiter just before dawn
So fat I think it's a helicopter hovering
Over bad traffic on the expressway
Until I look through my glasses
Good news for the morning commute
No tie ups on the Gowanus
A big planet in plain view
While we swing into sunlight

I push my father, not so old but frail
In a rolling recliner chair
On small wheels up a steep street
Bumping over sidewalk seams
As dusk falls and windows light

He gives me a tiny box, a kit
To make to make a matchbook house
Like Tinker Toy sticks the size of splinters
He warns me not to spill them

I leave him in his living room
On a low pallet beside a TV
He says we'll meet at the flea market

I carry two light cases of his odds and ends
Out into the night and unfamiliar blocks
Lost as it begins to rain but stops

I take a wrong turn up cemetery steps
And cannot get back down
For the crowds of people climbing

JANICE PARIAT

Greenwich

from October/November 2011

at the place where time begins and ends,
we search for spaces between lines,
watched by sunken-eyed skies,

piteously weeping. these trees
rising, watershed for lives that spill
over damp-dog grounds. what leaves,

green goslings shuddering in a sudden
river breeze, darkling bark that wraps
our insides, chaste with dripful longing.

at hilltop ruin, we crank up archaic
machinery—a sun follower at heart,
a cryptic medieval tunnel tossed

toward the discovery of stars.
at last, us alone through stone-gated
passage where the world is halved,

hung and quartered. we scramble
for direction, such pale, limpid light,
and wait for the enormity of thin,

invisible line to split our hearts.
love, such distances must separate
or kill with long, lingering hope.

MICHAELA A. GABRIEL

the secret meanings of greek letters: iota

from October/November 2006

the story of the fossil hunter in miniature letters:

hands turn every stone, heedless of rain, heat, hunger.
fingers decipher the braille of millennia—coils, antennae,
spores strewn like stars across the dark slate of sky.

the color of apple vinegar lures me to beaches for this:
a runaway drop of resin that caught an insect by surprise—
perfect legs, immaculate wings useless in their amber cage.

fingertips climb a spiral staircase to the center of a life
suspended in mid-air, my lips blow grains of sand from
ammonite folds; the voices of aeons rasp across my palm.

like linen awaits the needle to embroider what is plain,
the past, curled up in tight curves, waits for my skillful
touch to draw another story from those little deaths.

KEN POYNER

Familiarity

from July/August 2010

There is a lady raving on the roof.
It is dangerous for her to be up there:
The roof has an angle, not all
The tiles are even, and it is quite
A ways from the second story
To the flat, uncomforting lawn.
She gestures as though to draw her complaint,
Walks the spine of the roof as though
Years she has been a master roofer,
Knows how to keep gravity evenly split.
As we get closer, we can see
She is not all that steady, that distance
Made us assume she was doing well.
Her feet turn out, her legs quiver from the effort,
Half of her flailing is only a grasp for balance.
This will not end well. Closer still
We can tell she is not complaining,
That her gestures are simple instruments to draw
Us in, keep herself upright.
We are clearly in her fall zone now,
Can hear her uneven voice, understand
The unconditioned nature of her movement.
She is trying to tell us
There is a woman on the roof,
That she is that woman.

DANNY EARL SIMMONS

Darts

from January/February 2015

I tell myself
the memory
of a half-dozen welling red dots
along my little sister's back
before I was old enough
for kindergarten
is evidence
I've come a long way.

I tell myself that.

JOHN GROCHALSKI

bacon

from July/August 2010

outside the
butcher shop
at 78th
and 13th avenue
sits a pile
of skinned
pig carcasses
wrapped in plastic
they are stacked
one on top
of the other
pig upon pig
their bodies
spread out
they look like
leaping rabbits
or jumping sheep
the smell is outrageous
acrid and decaying
like a war zone
death on a spring
morning
there is one man
standing next to the pile
he is wearing

a bloody apron
and smoking
a cigarette against
the sun's light
he has a look of
utter apathy
on his face
this carnage means
nothing to him
but a paycheck
these pigs are
bacon frying
on a sunday morning
after a cold glass
of orange juice
while the church bells ring
for the holy
and the lost

J.P. DANCING BEAR

Gacela of Consumer Apathy

from July/August 2003

What I know about immunity is taught by the eyes
of sick caged rabbits, moving to heaven
for our vanity. My guilt is heavy as a brick.

I saw someone with rabbit eyes clutching a lipstick
like a carrot, behind boxes of cosmetics stacked
heavy as bricks, immune to heaven's light.

I was rabbit-punched by the brickly kiss
of glowing consumer angels, immune to responsibility,
who promised heaven in a sterile but pleasing wrapper.

My hand turning a heavenly radio dial, immune
to the rabbit-tongued announcers talking bric-a-brac
in a language of parsnips and bright flowers.

I sought diplomatic immunity in the City
of Rabbits, a heaven from the ravages of hawks,
a brick wall to block the language of feral dogs.

Under the brick facades all eyes turn upward,
almost in prayer, to the rabbit of the moon
immune to the cumulous heavens around it.

SARAH J. SLOAT

Headstone with Harvest Images

from January/February 2011

Flat at last, the grave finds antiquity
can be postponed no longer, and yesterday,
or last week, or that intricate winter

before the war, is past, all past,
with no gap between late and early.

There is comfort in the shape
of stone: the outcropping, dark marble

like a spoon, a solitaire set
in a ring, or an errant reference tab
referencing this single thing.

Dear wilderness, last night I dreamed
of an electric slumber,

a humming, buzzing kind of sleep,
poorly suffered, and this inscription is a wish
and a lie about peace,

which sits impossibly beside
engraved vines and wheat, and must
plod on beyond these oxen.

KATIE STEELE

Burrowing Frogs

from January/February 2013

Some days, our calls go unanswered.
Dry winds brush over our backs
and home is ebbing away. Everything has left:
the glint of the diving beetle, wavelets
over the surface, the swamphen's shadow.
All that remains are the turtle and snails
frozen in their torpor. These are our signs.
We dig into the mud, the slick of soil
against skin, caverns in the earth
filled with our bodies. All that's left
are heartbeats   slowing.

But living on emptiness isn't hard
if you are patient enough.
Beneath the ground the shifting of the world
has no bearing. Only bulbs and bodies
dampened by remnants of rain in the soil.
We know that the reeds are weaving roots
above us, that time moves without us.
When the wounds of our home have healed,
we will live again.

SRIYA NARAYANAN

Her Boy

from January/February 2010

Since the boy died, she's been haranguing
Priests, witches, doctors and Gods of various faiths
(But not Buddha who sends bereaved mothers
On a wild goose chase only to tell them
Their grief isn't unique).
She'll have you know
He was twelve and cheerful, especially
On his way back from school in the monsoon.
She watches him splatter about in shallow puddles
Secretly. Then, he's swallowed alive
In one hungry, smelly gulp.
Someone stole the manhole cover, she supposes.
There he goes, down the drain.
And to think just a moment ago
He was walking on water.

PATRICK KINDIG

Antecedent

from July/August 2014

Remember the backyards, the boys who lived
next door. Remember the geography

of names, the chain-link longitudes, the trees
and hedges with shadows hidden inside.

Remember summer, glistening bodies
sliding from the pool, tented sleepovers humid

with questions about skin asked and answered
with hands. Remember waiting. Remember

waiting more. Remember the way waiting
felt like it was the entire shining world.

JENNIFER VAN ORMAN YURGES

Holy Night

from April/May 2015

I am about six and from the front seat
Grandfather is yelling in Italian, which I don't understand
so it might as well be the priest's Latin prayer,
which I don't pay attention to either.

Speaking of which,
Grandmother is listening
to the rosary on cassette, Hail Marys under her breath,
and a cigarette burning in her bean bag ashtray.

Stubborn brat, mortal sin, bargain basement.
These are her favorite phrases.

Praying seems something designed
only to keep you up at night,
or like drinking orange juice with pulp,
something to be endured

and even by this age, I have learned to tune it out.
I know Grandfather isn't praying to Saint Christopher,
the patron saint of motorists, and she tells him
to shut his face, as the tape turns over again
like an insomniac.

I watch a green plastic rosary tangle around,
and dislike their God, angry as I am angry.
I sulk in the backseat but say nothing
as I am not to be heard. I hear this over and over
and, God, some nights I don't say anything at all.

CANDACE BUTLER

Clocks: No Time for a Funeral

from October/November 2014

I like grandfathers best,
so I can cut off their hands
when they steal time.
Their tics, they comfort me;
their impartial dial eyes,
partakers of flesh and blood.

Hear their longsuffering reputation:
footsteps, the *clink, clink, clink*
of Old Man Time and
his pocketful of dimes
dropping in the curse box
at the senior center.

JOEL FRY

Visitor

from January/February 2006

I come from the river,
where an abandoned pier
awaits collapse,
and water moccasins
slither through reflecting
dregs of flotsam.

I live alone.
Only five people remember
my name. Only one visits.

She fishes along the bank
behind my trailer. Sometimes
we speak.

Her face is as small
as a child's foot. Her eyes
are deserted isles.

When we meet,
she touches me
with the courtesy
of solitude, with the warmth
I stow on rainy days, with
the gaze I turn to in sleep.

JAROD K. ANDERSON

Better to Be Safe

from January/February 2012

When he thinks of it,
my father tries to talk over the rain
like his voice is a place of its own
where we won't see my mother
closing her eyes each time we pass
the great grey smudge of a semi.

When we have a quiet moment
in the safe places, she says the trucks
make her think of tasting her own blood,
like a penny on her tongue with one
cheek on the wet pavement
that should be cold, but isn't.

She tells me how the sky looks green
just before the tornado comes
and plucks the roof out into nothing
like the way black ice makes the brakes
useless, makes the steering wheel useless,
makes joints, tendons, muscles useless.

When they found her cancer,
she shaved her own head, standing
at the kitchen counter while my father
canceled their cruise ship reservations.

She waited for weeks to tell my brother
and me. She said I was too busy
for an extra worry.

SIMON PERCHIK

Untitled

from January/February 2011

Up was never the place, this bulb
brought down by the same gunfire
flickering for years on the ceiling

though the room stays empty
grieving for a side door to open
on where the sky used to be

—what you hear is a jacket
moving closer to the watch
still on your wrist reaching around

in your throat and overhead
you can hear its minutes
seconds and you count out loud

as if one sun still touches another
breaks apart in midair
colder than no place else or dark

—you hear the breath
that can only exhale, the gust
held close, frozen to your hand.

J. LADD ZORN, JR.

Coast Starlight, Northbound

from January/February 2015

Summerland
        (a sign points the way)
Palm trees rise
Over a rusted tin-roof barn
Where braceros stoop
In rows of strawberries
Outside of Oxnard;
Plastic-covered fields
Smokestacks in back
Odor of onions, though, there
Where the Tehachapis
Block the eastern horizon

Here now is the Pacific.
Ventura. Anacapa,
A dark form in the gloom,
River mouth, driftwood,
Feet from the sea.
Over a crumbling wall
Surfers clambered past
Stones rounded by waves over eons
Collected into fire pits,
Past clusters of deadwood,
Tangled like lost souls—
The Inferno open on my lap.

Contributors' Notes

Jarod K. Anderson has appeared in numerous online and print publications including *Daily Science Fiction, Escape Pod,* and *Apex Magazine*. His work is forthcoming in *Asimov's* and *Pseudopod*. His books of science fiction writing prompts (co-written with his wife Leslie J. Anderson) include: *Inklings: 300 Starts, Plots, and Challenges to Inspire Your Horror, Science Fiction and Fantasy* and *100 Prompts for Science Fiction Writers.*

Sandy Anderson has been published in *Weber Studies, Sugarhouse Review, Lucid Moon,* and *Limberlost Review*. She is the author of the book *At the Edge in White Robes* and a chapbook, *Jeanne Was Once a Player of Pianos*. Her poetry was recently published in the anthology *New Poets of the American West,* edited by Lowell Jaeger. She works as a piano teacher and is the founder of City Art, the longest-running reading series in Utah, and she was the editor of the literary magazine *Wasatch Front.*

Arlene Ang lives in Spinea, Italy. Her latest poetry collection is *Banned for Life*. She is also the author of *The Desecration of Doves, Secret Love Poems, Bundles of Letters Including A, V and Epsilon* (co-written with Valerie Fox), and *Seeing Birds in Church Is a Kind of Adieu*. Her poems have appeared in *Ambit, Caketrain, DIAGRAM, Poetry Ireland, Poet Lore, Rattle,* and *Salt Hill* as well as the *Dzank Best of the Web* 2008 and 2009.

Laird Barron spent his early years in Alaska, where he raced the Iditarod three times during the early 1990s and worked in the fishing and construction industries. He is the author of several books, including *The Imago Sequence, Occultation, The Beautiful Thing That*

Awaits Us All, and *Swift to Chase.* His work has also appeared in many magazines and anthologies. He now resides in the Hudson Valley writing stories about the evil that men do.

Kathryn T. S. Bass has been published in dozens of literary magazines and in three collections of poetry. She has taught creative writing to students of all ages, from pre-K to post-grad. Her honors have ranged from a blue ribbon at the Denver County Fair to a coveted State of Colorado Artist Fellowship. In recent years, she's earned juried residencies at both Brush Creek Ranch and the Jentel Foundation for the Arts. When not serving as an associate creative director or working on new writing projects, you'll likely find her gardening, practicing yoga, learning meditation, doodling, or enjoying time with her sweet husband and their two adorable dogs.

Ruth Baumann is a PhD student at Florida State University and holds an MFA from the University of Memphis. She's the author of three chapbooks: *I'll Love You Forever & Other Temporary Valentines, wildcold,* and *Retribution Binary* (forthcoming in 2017). Poems are published in *Colorado Review, Sonora Review, Sycamore Review, The Journal,* and *Third Coast.*

Kimberly L. Becker is the author of *Words Facing East* and *The Dividings.* A member of Wordcraft Circle of Native Writers and Storytellers, her poems appear in journals such as *Drunken Boat* and *Fulcrum* and in anthologies such as *Indigenous Message on Water* and *Bared.*

C. S. Bhagya is a D.Phil English scholar at the University of Oxford. Her writing has appeared in *Queen's Political Review, Muse India, The Ladies Finger,* and *Coldnoon: Travel Poetics.*

RK Biswas is the author of *Culling Mynahs and Crows, Breasts and Other Afflictions of Women,* and *Immoderate Men,* forthcoming from Speaking Tiger Books. Her short fiction and poetry have appeared in *Asia Literary Review, Per Contra, Etchings, Markings, Pushing Out the*

Boat, Muse India, Out of Print, and *Nth Position*. A Pushcart nominee, she won first prize in the Anam Cara Writer's Retreat Short Story Contest, second in the India Currents Katha Literary Fiction Prize, was a finalist in the Aesthetica Contest, and her novel was listed as one of the 20 most popular books of 2014 by The Readers' Club, Delhi.

Greta Bolger is a writer and artist living the dream in beautiful Benzonia, population 453. Her work has been published in *The Chimaera, Juice Box, Third Coast Magazine, Silver Birch Press,* and *The Literary Bohemian*. She paints imagined portraits and recently had her first acceptance into a juried show.

Nicole Borg has appeared in *Lake Region Review, Talking Stick, Lost Lake Folk Opera,* and *Nodin Poetry Anthology 2015*. In 2014, she received an Emerging Artist Grant from the Southeastern Minnesota Arts Council. Nicole is editor of *Green Blade*, the magazine of the Rural America Writers' Center. She lives in Wabasha, Minnesota, with her husband and two sons.

Brad Bostian is the Director of First Year Experience at a community college in North Carolina and the president of TYFY: Two Year First Year. He writes fiction in his spare time and poems mostly to his wife.

Bob Bradshaw is a big fan of the Rolling Stones and easy times. Mick may not be gathering moss, but Bob is. Bob hopes to retire to a hammock soon. His work can be found at *Cha, Pedestal, Stirring,* and *Rose and Thorn*.

Candace Butler is a poet and writer residing in the mountains of Appalachia in rural southwestern Virginia, where she is an Adjunct Professor of English at Emory & Henry College. She has published two chapbooks of poetry: *Royal Crown* and *Nothing Is So Lovely*.

Jared Carter is most recently the author of *Darkened Rooms of Summer: New and Selected Poems*. He lives in Indiana.

Rohan Chhetri is the author of *Slow Startle* (Winner of The (Great) Indian Poetry Collective's Emerging Poets Prize). His poems have been published or are forthcoming in *Vinyl, Fulcrum, Prelude, Rattle,* and *EVENT*. He was a 2016 Norman Mailer Poetry Fellow.

Antonia Clark is a writer, editor, and teacher, and co-administers an online poetry forum, *The Waters*. She is the author of a poetry chapbook, *Smoke and Mirrors*, and a full-length poetry collection, *Chameleon Moon*. Toni lives in Vermont, loves French picnics, and plays French café music on a sparkly purple accordion.

Lainey S. Cronk lives among immense oaks and winding roads in Northern California, where her work at an after-school program keeps her lively and inspired. She has worked at word-craft as a public relations writer, a freelance copyeditor, and a volunteer for non-profits, in addition to her on-going pursuit of poems. She has previously had poetry published in *Arsenic Lobster* and *Hotel Amerika*.

Rachel Dacus is a poet and writer whose recent book, *Gods of Water and Air*, combines poetry, prose, and drama. It follows two poetry collections, *Earth Lessons* and *Femme au Chapeau*. Her poetry, essays, stories, author interviews, and book reviews have appeared in *Atlanta Review, Boulevard, Drunken Boat, Fringe, The Pedestal, Valparaiso Poetry Review, Prairie Schooner*, and numerous anthologies. She grew up the daughter of a bipolar rocket scientist and artist in the southern California port town of San Pedro, migrated north to attend UC Berkeley in the interesting 60s, and never left the San Francisco Bay Area. She is at work on a time travel novel about the great Baroque sculptor Gianlorenzo Bernini.

Jesse Damiani is Series Editor of *Best American Experimental Writing*, the author of *@endless$pectator: The Screens Suite #sweetpicsbro #pixelated #loliloquy*, and Co-Founder of Galatea, a revolutionary pre-production tool for film, VR, AR, and MR storybuilding. The recipient of awards from the Academy of American Poets and the Fulbright Commission, his work has appeared in *The Adroit Journal,*

Barrow Street, Black Warrior Review, Colorado Review, and *North American Review.* A contributor to *Indiewire, UploadVR,* and *VRScout,* his poetry and criticism have been reprinted in *Verse Daily* and *CBS News.* He was the 2013-2014 Halls Emerging Artist Fellow at the Wisconsin Institute for Creating Writing, and now works in Los Angeles as a creative consultant, editor, and copywriter.

J.P. Dancing Bear is editor for the *American Poetry Journal* and Dream Horse Press. Bear is the author of 14 collections of poetry, the latest being *Cephalopodic* and *Love is a Burning Building.* His work has appeared in *American Literary Review, Crazyhorse,* and *Quarterly West.* In the second half of 2015, Bear and his wife, C. J. Sage, were named the editors of *Verse Daily.*

Barbara De Franceschi is an Australian poet from Broken Hill, a small mining town in outback New South Wales. Besides two collections of poetry, *Lavender Blood* and *Strands,* her work has appeared in anthologies and journals Australia wide, on-line, and in five other countries, as well as being featured on national radio. In her role as *Artist in Residence* for the New South Wales University Department of Rural Health, she encourages health science students to embrace creative writing as a means of enhancing communication, as a performance poet she entertains at community events and aged care facilities. Barbara was awarded the Order of Australia Medal in 2002 for her achievements in the area of multiculturalism.

Cy Dillon is a retired college librarian, editor, and writer who lives in the Virginia mountains.

Gary Dop is a poet, playwright, and performer who grew up throughout Germany and the Midwest. He now lives with his wife and three daughters in the foothills of the Blue Ridge Mountains, where he is an English professor at Randolph College. Dop's work has appeared in *Prairie Schooner, North American Review, Agni, PANK,* and *New Letters.* His first poetry collection is *Father, Child, Water.*

Noah Engel is an artist based in New York City. He graduated from New York University Tisch School of the Arts in the Film and Television Production Program with a Minor in Performance Studies. His work has been featured at *NYU First Run, LongHouse Reserve, DeepVimeo, Ross Gallery,* and *SDUFF.*

Chielozona Eze is a survivor of the 1967 Nigerian civil war. He grew up in Nigeria, where he studied philosophy and Catholic theology. He also studied philosophy, literature, and creating writing at Purdue University. He has published poems in several journals and chapbook, *Survival Kit.* He is associate professor of English, African, and African American Studies at Northeastern Illinois University.

Jennifer Finstrom has been the Poetry Editor of *Eclectica* since the fall issue of 2005. A former Spotlight Author, she teaches in the First-Year Writing Program, tutors in writing, and facilitates writing groups at DePaul University. Recent publications include *Autumn Sky Poetry Daily*, *Escape Into Life*, *NEAT.*, and *Gingerbread House Literary Magazine*. She also has work appearing in *The Great Gatsby Anthology*, the *Alice in Wonderland Anthology*, the *Nancy Drew Anthology*, and in *Ides: A Collection of Poetry Chapbooks*.

Brent Fisk is a writer from Bowling Green, Kentucky, with recent work appearing in *Lunch Ticket, Bat City Review*, and *Forge*. He has an MA in Creative Writing from Western Kentucky University.

Marc Frazier is a former *Eclectica* Spotlight Author who has published poetry in *The Spoon River Poetry Review, ACM, Good Men Project, f(r)iction, Slant, Permafrost, Plainsongs, Poet Lore, Rhino,* and *Connotation Press*. He has had memoir published in *Gravel* and *The Good Men Project* and forthcoming in *Evening Street Review* and *decomP*. He is the recipient of an Illinois Arts Council Award for poetry and has been featured on *Verse Daily*. His book *The Way Here* and his chapbooks *The Gods of the Grand Resort* and *After* are available on Amazon as well as his second full-length collection titled

Each Thing Touches. He has done readings and led workshops in the Chicago area for many years.

Joel Fry lives in Athens, Alabama. He has had poetry published in *Off the Coast, Iodine Poetry Journal,* and *Stirring*. He is seeking a publisher for his first book of poetry, *Getting Lost.*

Michaela A. Gabriel lives in Vienna, Austria, with her partner and 2 1/2-year-old daughter Emilia, who is the most fabulous reason why poetry has taken a back seat over the last few years. Previous publications include three chapbooks; the first full-length collection is patiently waiting to be picked up and finished.

Pamela Gemin was the editor of *Are You Experienced?* and the co-editor of *Boomer Girls: Poems by Women from the Baby Boom Generation*. Her first poetry collection was titled *Vendettas, Charms, and Prayers*, and her most recent book of poems is *Another Creature*, a finalist for the Miller Williams Poetry Prize. She lives in Flagstaff, Arizona.

Jude Goodwin is a founding member of the Squamish Writers Group and founder and co-editor of *The Waters*, an online poetry workshop. A former *Eclectica* Spotlight Author, she has placed well many times in the Internet Poetry Board Competition. She is pursuing a degree in Creative Writing with Douglas College, British Columbia, Canada.

Taylor Graham is a volunteer search-and-rescue dog handler in the Sierra Nevada, and serves as El Dorado County's first poet laureate (2016-2018). She's included in the anthologies *Villanelles* and *California Poetry: From the Gold Rush to the Present*. Her latest books are *What the Wind Says* and *Uplift*.

John Grey is an Australian poet living in the United States. Recently published in *New Plains Review, Stillwater Review*, and *Big Muddy Review,* with work upcoming in *Louisiana Review, Cape Rock,* and *Spoon River Poetry Review*.

John Grochalski is the author of *The Noose Doesn't Get Any Looser After You Punch Out, Glass City, In The Year of Everything Dying, Starting with the Last Name Grochalski*, and the novels, *The Librarian* and *Wine Clerk*. He lives in Brooklyn, New York, where the garbage can smell like roses if you wish on it hard enough.

Courtney Gustafson is a PhD candidate and writing instructor at the University of Massachusetts and a former *Eclectica* Spotlight Author. Her poetry and fiction have appeared in *Turk's Head Review, Jackson Hole Review, Sphere,* and *Misfit Magazine.*

Ruth D. Handel has published one poetry collection (*No Border Is Perennial*) and two chapbooks (*Tugboat Warrior* and *Reading the White Spaces*). After retiring as a professor, she is living an activist life with poetry: supporting others through teaching and mentorship; leading the Poetry Caravan, an organization bringing poetry to hospitals and shelters; reading her work in various venues; and trying to write poems reflecting issues of personal and political import.

Tim Hawkins has appeared in a number of notable print and online publications over the past decade, including *Blueline, Dogzplot, Iron Horse Literary Review, The Literary Bohemian, The Midwest Quarterly,* and *The Pedestal Magazine.* In 2012 he was nominated for a Pushcart Prize. His first poetry collection is *Wanderings at Deadline.*

L.I. Henley was born and raised in the Mojave Desert village of Joshua Tree, California. She is author of two chapbooks, *Desert with a Cabin View* and *The Finding,* and one full-length collection titled *These Friends These Rooms.* Her work has appeared in *RHINO Magazine, Arcadia, Askew,* and *Hayden's Ferry Review.* She is the recipient of the Academy of American Poets University Award, The Duckabush Poetry Prize, The Byzantium Poetry Prize, The Orange Monkey Publishing Prize, and the Poet's Billow Prize. She owns and edits *Aperçus Quarterly* with her husband, poet Jonathan Maule.

Margaret Holley is the former director of Bryn Mawr College's Creative Writing Program and now serves as a docent at Winterthur Museum. Her fifth book of poems is *Walking Through the Horizon.* Her work has appeared in *Poetry, Gettysburg Review, Shenandoah,* and *The Southern Review.*

Robert Hoover grew up in Binghamton, New York, graduated with a BA in English Literature from Binghamton University, and worked in the NYC magazine industry for 31 years. He has been painting in earnest for 12 years, work is about his emotional and sensual experiences.

Paul Hostovsky is the author of eight books of poetry, most recently *The Bad Guys,* which won the FutureCycle Poetry Book Prize for 2015. His poems have won a Pushcart Prize, two Best of the Net awards, The Muriel Craft Bailey Award from the Comstock Review, and chapbook contests from Grayson Books, Riverstone Press, Frank Cat Press and Split Oak Press. He has been featured on *Poetry Daily, Verse Daily, The Writer's Almanac,* and was a Featured Poet on the Georgia Poetry Circuit. His ninth full-length collection, *Is That What That Is,* is forthcoming in 2017. He makes his living in Boston as an interpreter at the Massachusetts Commission for the Deaf.

Lucas Jacob teaches writing for La Jolla Country Day School in California, and lives in Indianapolis, Indiana. His poems, essays, and stories have appeared in *Southwest Review, Barrow Street,* and *Hopkins Review.* His debut collection of poems is the chapbook *A Hole in the Light.*

Amy Crane Johnson is a former *Eclectica* Spotlight Author who has worked as a baker, a medical assistant, a vacuum cleaner sales rep, a children's book editor, and let us not forget, a mom and granny. She belongs to NEW Fiber Artisans and creates assemblages and lives in Green Bay, Wisconsin.

Patricia L. Johnson has appeared in *Foliate Oak, Apollo's Lyre, Southern Women's Review,* and *Ars Medica*. She was editor of *The Green Tricycle* online literary magazine for several years. She worked as an administrator for The Internet Writing Workshop. Her collection of flash fiction stories is *Destrehan and Other Tales*. She is searching for a publisher for her book of poems, *Prism Variation*.

Judy Kaber has appeared in *Ekphrasis, Off the Coast, The Comstock Review,* and *The Guardian*. Contest credits include the Maine Postmark Poetry Contest, the Larry Kramer Memorial Chapbook Contest, and, most recently, second place in the 2016 Muriel Craft Bailey Poetry Contest. She is a retired elementary teacher who enjoys reading, writing, and exploring Maine.

Aseem Kaul is an Assistant Professor at the University of Minnesota, where he teaches Strategic Management and Entrepreneurship. Aseem's work has appeared in T*he Missing Slate, DMQ Review, Night Train, Blood Orange Review,* and *The Cortland Review*. A collection of his short fiction, *études*, was published in 2009.

Elizabeth Kerper lives in Chicago and recently graduated from DePaul University with a BA in English literature. She is a contributing editor at *N/A Literary Magazine,* where her work has appeared. She is overly fond of avocados, rainy days, and the second person, and she can generally be found sitting quietly in the corner with her nose stuck in a book.

Patrick Kindig is a dual MFA/PhD candidate at Indiana University, where he studies American literature and writes poems. He's the author of the micro-chapbook *Dry Spell*, and his poetry has recently appeared in the *Beloit Poetry Journal, Willow Springs, the minnesota review,* and *Assaracus*.

Julie King lives in Albuquerque with eleven dogs, two children, one cat and one husband. When not untangling leashes, she's watching movies or teaching composition. Her work appears in the Iowa Press anthologies *Boomer Girls* and *are you experienced?*, and she has published in *Fiction International, Sundog, Puerto del Sol, Quarterly West, Gulf Coast,* and *Tin House*. She wrote, directed, and produced the short film *Worlds* and sometimes starred in B-horror movies. She first appeared in *Eclectica* in 1996 and was the poetry editor from 1999 to 2005.

Kathleen Kirk is the author of six poetry chapbooks, most recently *ABCs of Women's Work*, which contains the poem "Juncos" for the letter "J." Her work has appeared in *Arsenic Lobster, Menacing Hedge, Redheaded Stepchild, Fourth River,* and *Poetry East*. She is the poetry editor for *Escape Into Life*, an online magazine.

Ellen Kombiyil is the author of *Histories of the Future Perfect* and *avalanche tunnel*. She is a co-Founder of *The (Great) Indian Poetry Collective*, a mentorship-model poetry press publishing emerging voices from India/Indian diaspora. New work is forthcoming in *Boston Review, Drunken Boat, The Fiddlehead, The National Poetry Review* and *Prelude*.

Miriam Kotzin teaches creative writing and literature at Drexel University. *Debris Field*, her fifth collection of poetry, joins *The Body's Bride, Taking Stock, Weights & Measures,* and *Reclaiming the Dead,* along with a novel, *The Real Deal,* and a collection of flash fiction, *Just Desserts*. A collection of short fiction, *Country Music*, is scheduled for publication in 2017. Her poetry has appeared or is forthcoming in *Shenandoah, Boulevard, The Tower Journal, Mezzo Cammin*, and *Valparaiso Poetry Review*. She is founding editor of *Per Contra* and a contributing editor of *Boulevard*. Her poem "Albino" was previously anthologized in *The Body's Bride*.

Dorothee Lang is a freelancer, multilingual writer, and traveler. She lives in Germany and recently dealt with too many things that start with "c." She maintains a website called *blueprint21*.

William Lantry works in Washington, DC, and is editor of *Peacock Journal.* His collections are *The Terraced Mountain, The Structure of Desire* (winner of a 2013 Nautilus Award in Poetry), and a chapbook, *The Language of Birds.* He received his PhD in Creative Writing from the University of Houston. Honors include the National Hackney Literary Award in Poetry, Patricia Goedicke Prize, Crucible Editors' Prize, Lindberg Foundation International Poetry for Peace Prize (Israel), the Paris Lake Poetry Prize, and Potomac Review Prize.

Svetlana Lavochkina is a novelist, poet, and translator, born and educated in Ukraine, now residing in Germany. In 2013, her novella *Dam Duchess* was chosen runner-up in the Paris Literary Prize. Her debut novel, *Zap,* was shortlisted for Tibor & Jones Pageturner Prize 2015, slated for publication in the US in 2017. Svetlana's work has been published or is forthcoming *AGNI, New Humanist, Poem, Straylight, Circumference, Superstition Review, Witness, Drunken Boat,* and *Chamber Four Fiction Anthology.* Her experimental mono-musical, *Tumbleweed,* scored by Patrick Flanagan, was broadcast on *Radio Blau* in May of 2016.

Erika Lutzner is the author of three chapbooks with dancing girl press and has a chapbook out with Kattywompus Press. She also has a book out with Calypso Press called *While Everything Slipped Away from Me.* She is a former violinist and chef, living in Williamsburg, Brooklyn with her cat Neo and her boyfriend.

Aditi Machado is the author of two chapbooks, *Route: Marienbad* and *The Robing of the Bride.* Her first book of poems, *Some Beheadings,* will appear from Nightboat in 2017.

Mark Magoon is a poet, writer, and educator. He is the author of *The Upper Peninsula Misses You,* and he has been nominated for Best of the Net and the Pushcart Prize. He teaches writing at the University of Illinois at Chicago, reviews poetry for *Chicago Review of Books,* and makes home in the Windy City with his wife and their bulldog.

Clare L. Martin is a lifelong resident of Louisiana and edits *MockingHeart Review*. Her second collection of poetry, *Seek the Holy Dark*, is forthcoming in 2017. Her widely-acclaimed debut collection was *Eating the Heart First*. Martin's poetry has appeared in *Avatar Review, Blue Fifth Review, Thrush Poetry Journal, Melusine, Poets and Artists*, and *Louisiana Literature*. She has been nominated for a Pushcart Prize, Dzanc Books' Best of the Web, Best New Poets, and *Sundress'* Best of the Net.

David Mathews earned his MA in Writing and Publishing at DePaul University. His work has appeared in *After Hours, CHEAP POP, One Sentence Poems, OMNI Reboot, Word Riot, Silver Birch Press,* and *Midwestern Gothic.* His poetry was nominated for The Best of the Net and has received awards from the Illinois Women's Press and the National Federation of Press Women. He lives in his hometown of Chicago where he teaches and writes.

Sharon McDermott is a poet, musician, and literature teacher in a private school in Pittsburgh. She has published three chapbooks of poetry: *Voluptuous*, *Alley Scatting*, and *Bitter Acoustic*, that latter of which was chosen by the poet Betty Adcock as the 2011 Jacar Press chapbook winner. She is a recipient of both a Pittsburgh Foundation artist award and a PA Council on the Arts grant.

Mary Meriam was nominated for the 2015 Poets' Prize for her first collection, *Conjuring My Leafy Muse*. Her second collection, *Girlie Calendar,* was selected for the 2016 American Library Association Over the Rainbow List. Her poems have appeared in 12 anthologies, including most recently, *Measure for Measure: An Anthology of Poetic Meters*. Poems are published or forthcoming in *Literary Imagination, American Life in Poetry, Adrienne, Cimarron Review, Rattle, The New York Times, The Women's Review of Books,* and *Prelude.*

Jillian Merrifield has an MA in Writing and Publishing from DePaul University and is pursuing her PhD in English Studies at Illinois State

University. Her work has appeared in *Midwestern Gothic, NEAT., i CHEAP POP*, and she has been nominated for *Best of the Net*.

Marjorie Mir is a retired librarian, living in Bronxville, New York. She is a member of Poetry Caravan, a group of Westchester, New York, poets who share poetry with residents of care facilities. She has received two awards from *Atlanta Review*.

George Moore has published poems in *The Atlantic, Poetry, Colorado Reivew,* and *North American Review*. His recent collection, *Saint Agnes Outside the Walls*, was just released with FutureCycle Press. His earlier collections include *Children's Drawings of the Universe* and *The Hermits of Dingle*. He lives with his wife on the south shore of Nova Scotia.

Ranjani Murali is a Chicago-based writer and artist. She received her MFA in Poetry from George Mason University (GMU) and now teaches writing and literature at Harper College in Illinois. She is the recipient of fellowships from the Vermont Studio Center and the Fine Arts Work Center, and her poems and translations have appeared in *Phoebe, Word Riot,* and elsewhere. She won the Srinivas Rayaprol poetry prize in 2014, the inaugural Almost Island manuscript prize in 2015, and The Great Indian Poetry Collective's Editor's Choice award for her second manuscript.

Jack Murphy lives in Chicago.

Sriya Narayanan is a freelance writer and book editor from Chennai, India. She is also an animal welfare volunteer who helps find homes for shelter pets and other rescued animals through a newspaper column.

Kelly Nelson is the author of the chapbooks *Rivers I Don't Live By* and *Who Was I to Say I Was Alive*. She teaches Interdisciplinary Studies at Arizona State University.

David Oestreich is the author of the chapbook *Cosmophagy*. Recent poems have appeared in *Slippery Elm, The Findlay Courier, Stirring, A Literary Collection*, and *Windhover*. He lives in Northwest Ohio with his wife and three children.

Robert Okaji lives in Texas with his wife, two dogs, and some books. He is the author of the chapbook *If Your Matter Could Reform*, a micro-chapbook *You Break What Falls*, and *The Circumference of Other*, a chapbook-length piece included in *Ides: A Collection of Poetry Chapbooks*. His work has appeared or is forthcoming in *Boston Review, Panoply, riverSedge, High Window, Hermeneutic Chaos, Kindle Magazine, Glass, Clade Song, Four Ties Lit Review,* and *Otoliths*. His blog is called *O at the Edges*.

Janice Pariat is the author of *Boats on Land: A Collection of Short Stories* and *Seahorse: A Novel*. She was awarded the Young Writer Award from the Indian National Academy of Letters and the Crossword Book Award for Fiction. She lives in New Delhi, India.

Simon Perchik is an attorney whose poems have appeared in *Partisan Review, Forge, Poetry, Osiris,* and *The New Yorker*. His most recent collection is *Almost Rain*. More information, including free e-books and his essay titled "Magic, Illusion and Other Realities" is available on his website.

Leeann Pickrell lives in El Cerrito, California, where she works as a freelance editor, writes poetry and prose, and is also the managing editor of *Jung Journal: Culture & Psyche*. A former *Eclectica* Spotlight Author, she is working on a long essay about her experience in the 2004 Indian Ocean Tsunami.

Kenneth Pobo has a new book forthcoming from Circling Rivers Press called *Loplop in a Red City*. His work has appeared in *Hawaii Review, Cordite, Caesura,* and *Mudfish*.

Christine Potter is a poet and YA novelist who lives in a very old house out in the woods. She has appeared in *Rattle, The Raintown Review, The Crab Orchard Review, The Anglican Theological Review,* and *American Arts Quarterly*. Her two poetry collections are *Zero Degrees at First Light* and *Sheltering in Place*. The first two novels of her time travel trilogy, *The Bean Books,* are now available: *Time Runs Away with Her* and *In Her Own Time*. She has two spoiled tomcats and a patient husband.

Ken Poyner often serves as strange, bewildering eye-candy at his wife's power lifting affairs, where she is one of the most celebrated female power lifters of all time. His latest collection of short, wiry fiction, is called *Constant Animals*; his poetry of late has been sunning in *Analog, Asimov's, Poet Lore,* and *The Kentucky Review*; and his fiction has yowled in *Spank the Carp, Red Truck, Café Irreal,* and *Bellows American Review*. His own imprint, Barking Moose Press, is soon to release *Victims of a Failed Civics*, a book of poetry.

Arjun Rajendran has appeared in many publications, including *Star*Line, Berfrois, Strange Horizons, Elsewhere Lit, Mithila Review,* and *VAYAVYA*. He was a finalist for the 2012 *Atlanta Review* Poetry Award and one of three winners in the 2014 Red Ochre Chapbook Contest. *Snake Wine* was his first collection of poems.

Jessy Randall is a librarian at Colorado College. Her most recent book is *Suicide Hotline Hold Music*, a collection of poems and poetry comics.

John Reinhard is the author of two poetry collections, *On the Road to Patsy Cline* and *Burning the Prairie*. He earned his MFA from The University of Michigan where he received a Hopwood Award and Cowden Fellowship. A two-time winner of a Loft-McKnight Award in poetry, he lives in Owatonna, Minnesota, with his wife and their two tall children and teaches at South Central College in Faribault.

Penelope Scambly Schott won an Oregon Book Award for Poetry for her verse biography *A is for Anne: Mistress Hutchinson Disturbs the Commonwealth*. Her most recent book is *How I Became an Historian.* She lives in Portland and Dufur, Oregon, where she teaches an annual poetry workshop.

Tom Sheehan has published 28 books and has multiple work in *Rosebud, Linnet's Wings, Serving House Journal, Literally Stories, Copperfield Review, Literary Orphans, Indiana Voices Journal, Frontier Tales, Western Online Magazine, Faith-Hope and Fiction, Provo Canyon Review, Eastlit, Rope & Wire Magazine, The Literary Yard, Green Silk Journal, Fiction on the Web, The Path,* etc. Has 30 Pushcart nominations, 5 Best of the Net nominations (one winner). Recent publications: *Swan River Daisy* by *KY Stories, The Cowboys* by Pocol Press, and *Jehrico* by *Danse Macabre. Back Home in Saugus* is being considered, as is *Elements & Accessories*, and *Small Victories for the Soul.* He is 2016 Writer-in-Residence at *Danse Macabre* in Las Vegas.

Danny Earl Simmons is an Oregonian and a proud graduate of Corvallis High School. He is a friend of the Linn-Benton Community College Poetry Club and serves on the school's Poetry Advisory Committee. He is the author of a poetry chapbook entitled *The Allness of Everything*. He also assists the literary journal *Off the Coast* as a member of its editorial team.

Pooja Garg Singh is a US-based writer and poet. An IIM Lucknow alumna, she studied English Literature at Jesus and Mary College, New Delhi, and Print Journalism at Indian Institute of Mass Communication. *Everyday and Some Other Day* is her first collection of poems. Her translation of "Our Moon Has Blood Clots," Rahul Pandita's opus on Kashmiri Pandits, is forthcoming soon. Pooja is Reviews Editor for *Jaggery* and Poetry Editor for *Open Road Review.* She is also part of a motley group of story writers from India who write for radio, television, movies, and other media formats.

Sarah J. Sloat lives in Germany, where she works in news. Her poems and prose have appeared in *The Offing, Beloit Poetry Journal,* and *Linebreak*. If not at her desk, she is probably on the subway.

Pat Smith was incarnated from joy and confusion in France and raised beneath smokestacks in Ohio. His MFA is from NYU's Tisch School of the Arts, and he is the author of the play *Driving Around the House*. His poems have appeared in little journals you never heard of. He has always had very vivid dreams and believes it means something even though it doesn't pay very much. He works as an employee benefits advisor and is lucky enough to live with his wife, Susan, in Brooklyn, New York.

Alexandra Smyth lives in Brooklyn, New York. She is a graduate of the City College of New York MFA Creative Writing Program. Her work recently appeared or is forthcoming in *The Found Poetry Review, Rust + Moth*, and *Stirring*. She is the author of the forthcoming chapbook *The Things I Carried.*

Himali Singh Soin writes and performs poetry installations inspired by planetariness and the fantastic apocalypse, exploring alien distances and earthly intimacy, nativism, nationality, love across borders, and cultural flight. Recent performances include *In the Meantime* at The Royal Observatory, Greenwich, *The Abyss of Space* at The Mosaic Rooms, London, *The Clockmaker's Reverie* at Pi Artworks, London, *The Particle and the Wave* at Sector 2337, Chicago, *You really got me now* at Richmix London, *Transit* at Fabrika Moscow, *The Paris Follies* at The Meet Factory, Prague, and *Radar Level* at Kadist Foundation, San Francisco, and Khoj, Delhi. Her poetry has appeared in international journals, and she is a regular contributor to *Artforum* magazine. She lives and works in London and Delhi.

Katie Steele is an undergraduate student at Reed College in Portland, Oregon. Though she is working on a BA in Religion, she pursues creative writing in many different forms both in her academic and personal life. This was her first official publication, written while attending Chicago Academy for the Arts as a creative writing major.

Carolyn Stice is a former Spotlight Author. She is a writer, teacher, and activist. Her work has appeared in *Cutthroat, Painted Bride Quarterly, China Grove*, and *Permafrost*. She lives in northern New Mexico with her family and pets, where she enjoys hiking, camping, and avoiding poisonous animals.

Heather Styka is a Chicago songwriter and poet unafraid to go where others fear to tread. Beneath "sweet, soulful vocals" (*Portland Press Herald*) and "nimble fingerpicked guitar" (*Dispatch Magazine*) lie narratives of vulnerability, strength, and wanderlust. After graduating from DePaul University with a degree in creative writing, this young troubadour has performed for over a decade, released four full-length albums and a poetry collection, and toured from coast to coast. Her poetry has also been published in the *Worcester Review*.

Rohith Sundararaman is a poet based out of Mumbai, India. His work has been published in *Ghoti Mag, Two River Review, Right Hand Pointing, Asian Cha, Word Riot,* and *GUD Magazine*.

Ray Templeton is a former *Eclectica* Spotlight Author. A Scottish writer and musician, he lives in St. Albans, England. His writing, including poetry and short fiction, has appeared both in print and on the web, and sometimes even other people sing his songs. Recent work can be found in *nthposition, Left Hand Waving,* and *qarrtsiluni,* and in his e-chapbook *The Act Of Finding* and his collection of prose poems *The Skin Still Feels The Stone*. He is a regular contributor to *Musical Traditions* and a member of the editorial board of *Blues & Rhythm* magazine.

Scott Urban has either recently appeared or is scheduled to appear in *Burning Word Journal, 2 Rivers View,* and *The Horror Zine*. His dark short fiction is collected as *Bloody Show*. His most recent poetry collection is *God's Will*. His most recent anthology is in *Every River* *on Earth.* He lives and writes in southeastern Ohio in a former Amish farmhouse that isn't haunted... yet.

Frank Van Zant directs the Greenhouse Alternative Program for high school kids in Rockville Centre, New York. With more than 400 credits, he was a featured poet in *The Chiron Review* and is the author of *Climbing Daddy Mountain* and *The Lives of the Two-Headed Baseball Siren*, the latter of which has occupied a spot in the Baseball Hall of Fame since 2008.

Michael VanCalbergh is a graduate of the Rutgers-Newark MFA in Poetry. He teaches writing and comics in New Jersey when he is not convincing his daughter that she needs shoes. His work has appeared in *The Collagist, Per Contra,* and *Apex.* He is also one half of the etymology/humor podcast *Words for Dinner.*

Mihir Vatsa is the author of the poetry collection *Painting That Red Circle White.* Winner of the Srinivas Rayaprol Poetry Prize and a former Charles Wallace Fellow of Writing at University of Stirling, he lives in Noida, India, where he works for a non-profit organization.

Teresa White was born and raised in Seattle and has been published over 100 times in online and print journals. She has received two Pushcart nominations. Her latest book, "Gardenias for a Beast," was nominated for the Pulitzer in 2007. Retired, she spends time online participating as a member of the Wild Poetry Forum. When not writing, she is busy with her second love, watercolor painting.

Shannon Connor Winward is the author of the Elgin-award winning chapbook, *Undoing Winter.* Her poems have appeared in places like *The Pedestal Magazine, Analog, Literary Mama, Hip Mama, Rogue Agent*, and *Thank You For Swallowing.* In between writing, parenting, and other madness, she is also a poetry editor for *Devilfish Review* and founding editor of the forthcoming *Riddled with Arrows Literary Journal.*

Laura Madeline Wiseman teaches at the University of Nebraska-Lincoln. Recent books are *An Apparently Impossible Adventure* and, with artist Chuka Susan Chesney, *People Like Cats*. She is also the author of *Drink*, winner of the 2016 Independent Publisher Bronze Book Award, and *Intimates and Fools* with artist Sally Brown Deskins, an Honor Book for the 2015 Nebraska Book Award. Her essay on long distance cycling, "Seven Cities of Good," is an honorable mention for the *Pacifica Literary Review's* 2015 Creative Nonfiction Award.

Tara Wynne (fka Tara Gilbert-Brever) wrote poems "back in the day," some of which were published in *Primavera, Stirring, The Blue Moon Review, Wicked Alice, small.spiral.notebook*... Now she lives next door to her childhood home with her husband and two young children. To satisfy that creative gnaw, she focuses on creating fiber arts, photography, and pyrography.

Grzegorz Wróblewski was born in 1962 in Gdansk and grew up in Warsaw. Since 1985 he has been living in Copenhagen. He is the author of many books of poetry, drama, and other writings. As a visual artist, he has exhibited his paintings in various galleries in Denmark, Germany, England, and Poland. English translations of his work are available in *Our Flying Objects*, *A Marzipan Factory*, *Kopenhaga*, and *Let's Go Back to the Mainland*.

Sarah Yost is a National Board certified teacher of early adolescent English language arts. She teachers eighth grade in Oldham County, Kentucky, and serves in district, regional, state and national teacher leadership roles. She loves to read and write, especially with her young son, William.

Jennifer Van Orman Yurges lives in Hallowell, Maine. She received an MFA in Creative Writing from University of Southern Maine in 2007.

J. Ladd Zorn, Jr. has a BA from UC Irvine, an MS from Walden University, and a Certificate in Fiction Writing from UC Riverside. His stories and poems have appeared in *Inlandia, Phantom Seeds, The Speculative Edge, Down in the Dirt Magazine's* online and print editions, *Hello Horror*, *Nth Position Online,* and *Floyd County Moonshine*. He is seeking a publisher for his novel *Internal Combustion* about a Disneyland Goofy who becomes a gun runner.

Recommended Online Poetry Publications

3:AM Magazine
Arsenic Lobster
Atticus Review
Autumn Sky Poetry
Blackbird
Blue Fifth Review
Blue Heron Review
the blueshift journal
Cider Press Review
Connotation Press
damselfly press
Diode
Escape Into Life
Eunoia Review
FreezeRay Poetry
FRiGG
Gingerbread House
Literary Orphans
Menacing Hedge
MockingHeart Review
Neat.
One Sentence Poems
Rose Red Review
Silver Birch Press
Sundress Publications
Thrush
Yellow Chair Review
Yew Journal

www.ingramcontent.com/pod-product-compliance
Lightning Source LLC
Chambersburg PA
CBHW061820040426
42447CB00012B/2743
9780996883016